PREACHING THAT CONNECTS

PREACHING THAT CONNECTS

Using the Techniques of Journalists to Add Impact to Your Sermons

MARK GALLI AND CRAIG BRIAN LARSON

ZondervanPublishingHouse

Grand Rapids, Michigan

A Division of HarperCollinsPublishers

Requests for information should be addressed to:
  Zondervan Publishing House
  Grand Rapids, Michigan 49530

Library of Congress Cataloging-in-Publication Data
Galli, Mark.
        Preaching that connects : using the techniques of journalists to add
    impact to your sermons / Mark Galli and Craig Brian Larson.
            p.   cm.
    Includes bibliographical references.
    ISBN 0 – 310 – 38621 – 7 (softcover)
        1.   Preaching.   2.   Communication — Religious   aspects —
    Christianity. I. Galli, Mark. II. Title
    BV4211.2.L375   1994   94 – 9870
    251 — dc20   CIP

Edited by Elizabeth Yoder

Printed in the United States of America

98 99 /❖ DH / 10 9 8 7 6 5

To Ernest Iden Bradley,

>who took a chance on an unexperienced young man, giving him his first opportunity to preach.

>—MARK GALLI

To Marvin Fulks,

>who nurtured men as a preacher,

and to Jim Hall,

>who taught me to study the Word.

>—BRIAN LARSON

Contents

Acknowledgments

Special thanks to Marshall Shelley and the editors of *Leadership* journal and Christianity Today, Inc., for sharpening our journalistic skills and for exposing us to the array of great preachers featured on *Preaching Today*.

Thanks also to those who have granted permission to use extensive quotations from sermons:

Excerpts from the sermon "When Life Crowds You Out" by Bruce Thielemann are used in chapter 3 with the permission of Mrs. Alyce Thielemann.

Excerpts from the sermon "Why I Believe in the Church" are used in chapter 10 with the permission of Jay Kesler.

Excerpts from the sermon "The Hard Side of Epiphany" are used in chapter 10 with the permission of Fred B. Craddock.

Foreword

George MacLeod of the Iona Community related a conversation that he had with a Marxist who had never heard an explanation of basic Christianity. The man listened with wonder and surprise. Finally, he burst out, "You folk have got it; if only you knew you had it, and if only you knew how to say it!"

Knowing "how to say it" is not incidental to preaching; it is crucial. Today's would-be communicator speaks as a small voice in an alphabet of voices. The preacher contends with ABC, CBS, NBC, CNN, ESPN, PBS, A and E, and MTV.

Not only do modern ministers have to lift their voices above the crowd, but they compete with major leaguers highly skilled in going after an audience. Communication isn't what it used to be. Any effort to foist dull, tired, jargon-filled material on readers or listeners meets with irritation or, worse, disdain.

Preachers address an audience that comes to church with clickers in their heads. In modern culture, people distinguish quickly between the interesting and the tedious. They scan the newspaper for stories that catch their minds. They flip through magazines and read the first sentence or the opening paragraph to decide whether it "sounds interesting." They vote in the first thirty seconds whether to tune in or turn off the channel.

Women sit in the congregation with thoughts half on the words and half on the tensions at the office. Men sit in the audience wishing they had a seat for the football game blacked out on local television. Teenagers sprawl in the pew thinking about getting a driver's license and sorting out the prospects of what to do with their Sunday afternoon. All of them look up at the pastor, but that does not mean they are listening. That lonely figure in the pulpit may have what the folks in front of him need, but they won't listen unless he knows how to say it.

Fortunately, he doesn't have to do it alone. The Holy Spirit stands there with him. What is more, God has given writers like Mark Galli and Brian Larson the gifts, experience, and insights for getting the message across effectively. In this book, *Preaching That Connects,* they share what they know with those of us who have something to say and want to say it well. They write simply and clearly. The pages are loaded with specific, geared-to-the-pulpit suggestions that can make the good news about Jesus sound more urgent than the evening news with Peter Jennings.

Preaching That Connects takes only a couple of hours to read and gives a lifetime of benefit.

— HADDON ROBINSON

Preface

Preachers who have studied homiletics in seminary quickly find out, once in a church pulpit, that homiletical and hermeneutical precision does not necessarily make for captivating sermons. Some follow the rules but bore their listeners. Meanwhile, they listen to the Chuck Swindolls and Bill Hybelses of the world, covet the ability to communicate, but don't know how Swindoll and his kind do it.

One answer, we've found, lies in another discipline: journalism. Interesting, captivating communication is what journalism is all about. If pastors want to learn how to communicate, they will find many of the best lessons in the principles that guide engaging writers of both nonfiction and fiction. These lessons, as practiced by today's better preachers, make up the chapters of this book.

Both of us were pastors and preachers, and both moved from there to work as editors for *Leadership* journal. We've discovered that the more we've learned about writing, the better we've preached. Since journalism concerns itself with the art of communicating, our improved preaching makes sense.

This book, therefore, could also be called *Journalistic Preaching,* for it will look at preaching in light of the well-accepted maxims of good writing.

To get the most out of this book, two assumptions are critical:

First, we assume that readers have some background in exegesis and traditional homiletics. The suggestions in this book are shallow if the preacher is not a disciplined student of the Word and of preaching.

Second, we assume that the reader first and foremost depends on the Holy Spirit to empower the preaching moment. The techniques we share are just that, techniques that have proven helpful to those who want to communicate. But techniques cannot change hearts. Techniques cannot make disciples. Only the presence of Christ in preaching can do that.

Our goal is to follow in the footsteps of Paul and Barnabas, who at Iconium "spoke so effectively that a great number of Jews and Gentiles believed" (Acts 14:1).

1

Love Your Hearers As Yourself

I once slammed a junior high boy against a chalkboard. I was the youth minister of a suburban church in California. Todd, a gangly mass of energy with wild, blond hair, had been darting around the room, playfully harassing other boys, oblivious to my instructions. He was, in short, acting like a junior high boy. The problem was he always acted like this. At every meeting. For the entire meeting.

On this chilly autumn night, after I asked Todd to sit down for the fifth time and he didn't, I decided I had had it with the little twerp. I grabbed his shoulders, spun him around, and pinned him against the wall.

"That's enough screwing around!" I screamed. I'd been wanting to say that for weeks.

"But Mark," he broke in, "I thought — "

"I don't give a rip what you think! When I tell you to do something, you do it! *DO YOU UNDERSTAND ME?*"

The room was very still; the clock ticked; warm air pushed through the heating ducts. Todd, his eyes wide in disbelief, nodded.

I let him go and composed myself. "Okay," I said as if nothing extraordinary had happened, "how about getting back to our activity." Everyone, including Todd, was remarkably cooperative.

Afterwards, the college-aged sponsors affirmed me for my strong leadership. A few meetings later, one of the boys told me he thought Todd had it coming that night. But I felt awful for weeks. I think Todd did too; I didn't see much of him after that.

I regret that episode not simply because I lost Todd, but because it came to symbolize so much of my later ministry with adults. Not that I lost my temper again (maybe once), but this episode revealed something of my fundamental attitude toward people when I began preaching.

DO YOU UNDERSTAND ME?

The problem with most parishioners is that they act like parishioners. They skip worship if they get tickets to a Cubs' double header. They read Peretti and Swindoll more than they read their Bibles. They squeeze prayer between appointments, if they pray at all. They remember jokes, not sermon outlines.

In other words, people act like sinners. As their pastor, that irked me. I had so much they needed to know, so much they needed to do, and they just didn't take it seriously enough.

So every once in a while, I would slam them against the wall with a "prophetic" sermon: "I've had enough of your behavior! Start acting like Christians!" by which I meant, "Act more like me!" (someone who had given his whole life to the church). Finally, in one way or another, I would end up saying, with just a touch too much irritation, "Do you understand me?"

Actually, these admonishments were often well-received. Such preaching excites the blood. There's something cathartic about groveling in guilt for a while. We walk away feeling like we've paid for our sins. And for a few weeks, people were better disciples. Then again, some people I didn't see much after that.

After a few such sermons, I saw I was not getting through. The congregation just didn't get it. Perhaps in a television age, preaching no longer worked, despite biblical teaching to the contrary.

The problem, of course, was not preaching. To paraphrase G. K. Chesterton: it was not that preaching had been tried and found wanting; it had not been tried. I had not tried real preaching, preaching that loves.

My exasperation revealed that lack. I was concerned mostly with *understanding*. But people are more than minds, and if I was to love them, my preaching had to touch more than their brains. I discovered I was more interested that people hear *my* concerns, *my* insights, and *my* exegesis of the gospel than that I speak about their concerns in a way that would help them experience the gospel.

In short, I preached as if I didn't love my parishioners. I have since learned that I wasn't alone — a lot of preachers struggle to love their hearers as themselves. I have also since learned what loving preaching might look like.

SELF-DENIAL

Julie, an angular woman with piercing eyes behind round, wire-rimmed glasses, asked sharp questions and made even sharper comments when she sat in my adult Sunday school class. She was never mean-spirited, but she and her husband, both Cambridge graduates, insisted on precision of thought. Their presence "encouraged" thorough preparation on my part.

I once asked Julie to lead a few sessions of the adult class. She complied, after warning that she wasn't a good teacher.

When I asked her to explain, she said, "I like to teach a subject more than I like to teach people."

Upon leaving seminary, and for many years hence, the preacher is full of aorist tenses and Q, the glories of prelapsarianism and the evils of Arianism. Preaching is a desperate struggle to get this knowledge out of our systems. Partly, we need to justify the money we spent learning that stuff. Partly, we really think that stuff is interesting — and we can't imagine that others won't find it as interesting. It really gets bad when we start thinking the congregation *needs* to know that stuff in order to be mature in Christ.

We love the subject more than our people.

It doesn't take many annual reviews to see that our preaching isn't connecting, and the usual complaint is that we "don't use enough illustrations."

That's a little annoying because the pure Word of God, expressed as cogently as we express it, should be enough for mature Christians. But we're becoming realists, so we subscribe to an illustration service and start keeping files of stories and articles (and a few jokes).

So now, in addition to our other pastoral duties, and in addition to the hours spent in exegesis and theological application, we need to carve out time to add illustrations and quotes and the like. After a few weeks, we protest: *What a waste! Why do I have to entertain people? Isn't the Word of God enough?*

We're more interested in the subject than in the people.

The first act of love in preaching is an act of self-denial — to become more interested in people than in the subject. That means giving up the love of knowledge and replacing it with a love for people.

We need to learn to put our knowledge in the service of the people, in terms and ways they can appreciate, not because we have to oversimplify the message, but because we love people so much that we'll do whatever it takes to communicate with them.

Journalists, whose business is communication, cannot write or edit to their own tastes. Editors read more manuscripts and articles in one month than most people read in a year. They can easily become cynical after a few years because hardly anything they read is fresh.

But they cannot choose and edit articles based on their own experiences. They have to keep the reader in mind, and what may not be fresh and interesting to seasoned editors will be new to readers. A good editor edits by a simple but effective motto: The reader first.

Preachers would do well to preach by a similar motto: Hearers first. More to the point, we need to learn how to introduce, develop, and conclude our subjects in a way that interests hearers. That means we need to learn how to craft sentences, paragraphs, stories, and illustrations for maximum impact.

This requires learning new skills. And that requires self-denial.

INTEREST IN THE WHOLE PERSON

I love my wife, and I often tell her so in a plain, unadorned way: "Honey, I love you," or "I appreciate how much you do for me." And sometimes I list reasons why I'm thankful for her. These are straightforward, rational expressions of my love.

But my wife needs more, and I want to communicate more — I want her to know in her heart that I love her. So I regularly (though not regularly enough) try to reach her heart. I hold her in my arms for a few minutes each morning. I buy her roses from time to time. I pick out romantic greeting cards and write her notes.

Sometimes I think, *Do I really have time to do this today? She knows I love her.* But only in her head. Unless I take the trouble to do the things that reach her heart, she just won't "get it."

In preaching, we give hugs, roses, and romantic greeting cards to our congregations when we use language in a way that speaks not only to our hearers' minds, but also to their hearts. And it is absolutely vital that we do so.

Philosopher John MacMurray put it this way: "What we feel and how we feel is far more important than what we think and how we think. Feeling is the stuff of which our consciousness is made, the atmosphere in which all our thinking and all our conduct is bathed. All the motives which govern and drive our lives are emotional. Love and hate, anger and fear, curiosity and joy are the springs of all that is most noble and most detestable in the history of men and nations."[1]

He may overstate the case but not by much. Right thinking is crucial, but as MacMurray argues, so is right feeling. Ian Pitt-Watson, preaching professor at Fuller Theological Seminary, notes what every preacher soon discovers: "The truth of the Faith is something that is felt rather than thought by many deeply committed Christian people. . . . Many in our congregation who think unreliably about their faith feel authentically about it."[2]

If we care about our people, we will have to touch this central part of their beings when we preach.

GETTING THE GOSPEL ACROSS

When he wanted to say, "God forgives you," Isaiah wrote,

Though your sins are like scarlet,
   they shall be as white as snow;
though they are red as crimson,
   they shall be like wool. (Isaiah 1:18)

When he wanted to show Israel how much God loved them, Hosea quoted the Lord, saying,

When Israel was a child, I loved him,
   and out of Egypt I called my son. . . .
It was I who taught Ephraim to walk,
   taking them by the arms;
but they did not realize
   it was I who healed them.
I led them with cords of human kindness,
   with ties of love;
I lifted the yoke from their neck
   and bent down to feed them. (Hosea 11:1 – 4)

When he wanted to say, "We have been called into the church by grace," Paul wrote,

Brothers, think of what you were when you were called. Not many of you were wise by human standards; not many were influential; not many were of noble birth. But God chose the foolish things of the world to shame the wise; God chose the weak things of the world to shame the strong. He chose the lowly things of this world and the despised things — and the things that are not — to nullify the things that are, so that no one may boast before him. (1 Corinthians 1:26 – 29)

Instead of defining terms and outlining arguments to clarify his message, Jesus said, "A farmer went out to sow his seed . . . " and "A man was going down from Jerusalem to Jericho . . . " and "There was a man who had two sons . . . "

Bible scholars commonly point out that the biblical message is intended for the whole person, that salvation touches heart, soul, mind, and strength. What is less noticed is that for the biblical writers, the medium is the message. They understood that if they wanted to communicate a holistic salvation, they needed to use holistic means. For the biblical writers, that meant using language to its fullest.

Pitt-Watson writes, "Intellect and will alone may hear the Law preached but not the gospel. The intellect may accept the truth of what is said, and the will may strive to act upon it; but until the emotions assent to the intellect, they will labor and, even if the gospel is preached, only the Law will be heard. You can see this happening in our churches when you look at a sea of impassive faces."[3]

What is true of biblical writers has also been true of the great preachers in Christian history. They knew how to employ language to affect hearers; they knew the ancient art of rhetoric.

For example, Augustine, the great theologian of the fifth century, was a renowned teacher of rhetoric before he converted to Christianity. Applying his communication skills to preaching and teaching his new faith, Augustine, the Christian rhetorician, defined the preacher's task as *docere, deletare, flectere* — to teach, to delight, to influence. To touch the mind, the heart, the will.

As a cursory study of their preaching shows, Chrysostom, Luther, Whitefield, and Spurgeon, among a host of other great preachers, all followed Augustine's advice. They knew how to use language to communicate felt truths. They knew instinctively what Pitt-Watson declares: "Unless there is some measure of emotional involvement on the part of the preacher and on the part of his hearers, the *kerygma* cannot be heard in its fullness, for the *kerygma* speaks to the whole man, emotion and all, and simply does not make sense to the intellect and will alone."[4]

THE LANGUAGE OF LOVE

For many people, the word *rhetoric* suggests something phony, something added to speech by those who wish to manipulate or grab for attention. It is "mere" rhetoric, hardly essential to the message.

For us, however, employing rhetoric simply means using language to its fullest, attempting with words to affect heart, mind, soul, and strength. To us, this is an act of love. And this is essential to the message.

Still, those suspicious of rhetoric are suspicious for good reason. We are wise to be aware of three temptations when we start using language to its fullest.

First, mere technique can draw undue attention to itself. The warnings of C. H. Spurgeon about oratory, the sister of rhetoric, apply not only to inappropriate mannerisms but also to self-serving rhetoric:

> I hope we have forsworn the tricks of professional orators, the strain for effect, the studied climax, the prearranged pause, the theatric strut, the mouthing of words, and I know not what besides, which you may see in certain pompous divines who still survive upon the face of the earth. May such become extinct animals ere long, and may a living, natural, simple way of talking out of the gospel be learned by us all; for I am persuaded that such a style is one which God is likely to bless.[5]

Second, a studied use of language can draw undue attention to the preacher. Scottish preacher James Denney put it this way: "No man can bear witness to Christ and himself at the same time. No man can at once give the impression that he is clever and that Christ is mighty to save."[6]

So, rhetoric, as well as oratory, can be phony, pompous, hypocritical, and ultimately self-defeating. But the solution is not to give up the studied use of language. As Richard John Neuhaus puts it, "Oratory that sounds pompous is bad oratory; rhetoric that sounds contrived is bad rhetoric; the antidote for both is better oratory and better rhetoric."[7]

CRASS MANIPULATION OR LOVING LEADERSHIP?

One of the most powerful sermons I've ever read is full of exegetical and logical flaws. It is so powerful that I didn't notice the near complete disregard for the text until, in preparation for this book, I had read the transcript half a dozen times. It was a masterpiece of rhetoric. It was miserable exegesis.

It struck me afresh how dangerous good rhetoric can be — if we aren't careful and conscientious with the truth and fully committed to God's purposes in our preaching. This is the third caution we should keep in mind. You can build a sermon on poor exegesis and illogic and, by means of rhetoric, captivate an audience and gather a following. You can influence people in a merely human way. You can even successfully propagate lies, as did Adolf Hitler.

This is one reason why many preachers have been hesitant about rhetoric, starting with Paul:

> When I came to you, brothers, I did not come with eloquence or superior wisdom as I proclaimed to you the testimony about God. For I resolved to know nothing while I was with you except Jesus Christ and him crucified. I came to you in weakness and fear, and with much trembling. My message and my preaching were not with wise and persuasive words, but with a demonstration of the Spirit's power, so that your faith might not rest on men's wisdom, but on God's power. (1 Corinthians 2:1 – 5)

We want people to be touched by the Spirit, not by our language. Yet ironically, the passage above is effective precisely because of Paul's use of language. For example, he employs hyperbole: "I resolved to know *nothing* except Jesus Christ and him crucified." That may have been his highest goal, but it obviously wasn't his only goal — we can assume he grounded his message in the resurrection as well.

He also uses parallelism: "eloquence or superior wisdom," "Jesus Christ and him crucified," "My message and my preaching," "wise and persuasive."

And he employs contrast: "not with wise and persuasive words, but with a demonstration of the Spirit's power," "that your faith might not rest on men's wisdom, but on God's power."

In short, the very passage that seems to castigate rhetoric is itself a model of rhetoric. Add to that the passage that comes just before it ("Not many of you were wise by human standards; not many were influential; not many were of noble birth . . . ") and the soaring chapter on love, 1 Corinthians 13, to name two — it's clear that Paul is no plain speaker.

The question is not whether our communication is manipulative. Of course it is manipulative — in the good sense. We want to influence, shape, alter, change how people think and behave — but not for personal gain. We do not want to be deceptive. We do not want to get people so emotionally charged they'll do anything we say. We do not want to overpower people's free wills. But we do want to influence people.

The key question is this: What will we influence them for? For our agendas? Or for Christ's? Rhetoric is like fire: it can burn and destroy; but when used in love, it can bring warmth and light.

It is our highest aspiration to bring the warmth and light of Christ's love to people. We want nothing less than to affect the whole person with the whole gospel. To that end we have given ourselves to studying how to use language to its fullest, looking especially at effective communicators today — preachers and writers — and analyzing what exactly they do to affect both mind and heart.

The following chapters contain some of the results of that study.

2

How to Be More Creative

Preachers face a bracing challenge: to proclaim the millenni-ums-old Scriptures in a way that never grows musty. We can say nothing really new, but it must seem new. Like a resourceful cook finding different ways to whip up a plate of meat and potatoes, we must proclaim the familiar gospel in unfamiliar ways, week after week (perhaps two to five times a week), month after month, year after year. Clearly, the creative demand on a pastor makes working as a restaurant chef on Mother's Day look easy.

Anything pastors can do, then, to enhance their creative abili-ties eases this crushing load. Certainly, our dependence on prayer and the inspiration of the Holy Spirit is the basis for our creativity, yet that does not nullify the human dimension. By our work habits and mind-set, we hinder or heighten inspiration.

Writers, who keep pasta on the table by selling manuscripts, have the same urgent need for ideas. For centuries writers have probed the so-called "muse," the mystery of inspiration. Today, in our scientific age, they have focused their attention on the growing field of research into creativity.

For several decades researchers have asked: How do fertile minds — particularly "geniuses" in various fields — generate ideas?

Do they have anything in common? Can others, especially communicators, learn from them?

According to these researchers, the answer is yes.

This chapter explores practical ways to overcome "preacher's block," to get ideas gushing. We will look at a method of sermon writing that takes advantage of what researchers have learned about creative people. And we will highlight the mind-set that is the fertile soil of germinating ideas.

INCOMPATIBLE THINKING

There are two types of thought processes essential to creativity, and they are mutually incompatible: generative thinking and evaluative thinking. Like a tree sprouting buds, leaves, and branches, generative thinking multiplies ideas, images, observations, principles, insights. Like a gardener pruning branches, evaluative thinking severs unwanted growth, useless ideas.

Generative thinking adds and multiplies; evaluative thinking subtracts and divides.

To write a sermon, we employ both thought processes, but each works best when the other is dormant. (Realistically, we don't do one or the other exclusively, but one dominates.) We generate the most ideas when we aren't testing whether each new thought is true, logical, relevant, or important. Evaluative thinking is a hostile environment for new life. Conversely, we evaluate ideas best when we stop mental seed-proliferation and cultivate what we have — categorizing, organizing, and deleting.

In the beginning, during what should be the generative phase of sermon preparation, we are most likely to suffer preacher's block. Timothy Perrin, in his article "Unleashing Your Creativity: Becoming a Better, More Productive Writer," summarizes five techniques that invigorate our generative, inventive thought processes: freewheeling, clustering, heuristics, conversation, and outlining.[1]

Freewheeling is an unstructured approach that frees us from the tyranny of our critical minds. For example, try this exercise: For five to ten minutes, write down anything and everything that comes to mind about your subject with no concern whatsoever for its usefulness. Don't stop or pause; don't correct spelling or grammatical errors. If you can't think of anything to say, repeat the last word until a new thought surfaces. The primary goal is to jump-start your generative thinking. If useful thoughts result, all the better.[2]

Clustering, or mind mapping as some call it, explores thought associations. For example, write your subject in the center of a sheet of paper and circle it. Then let your mind roam free on the subject. As words, images, Scriptures, stories, memories, people, and principles surface in your mind, write them down (in a word or phrase at most), circle them, and draw a line from the central idea to the new word bubble. As that bubble in turn triggers further ideas, extend the network, radiating ideas from the subject hub.

When you are finished, pick the useful fruit from the tree. The ideas that don't fit your plans now may come to mind in useful ways later when writing the sermon.[3]

A *heuristic* (from the Greek word *heuriskein,* "to find out") is a list of questions. A heuristic gives more tangible guidance to our imagination than freewheeling and clustering, and may be our best resort when we're not only blocked but barricaded. Homiletics books often contain such lists,[4] but to fit your style and tendencies, and to compensate for weaknesses, you might develop your own.

Some of the following questions may prove useful in your personal heuristic:

- Whom am I speaking to?
- How should this text affect the way my listeners live tomorrow?
- What are the word pictures in this text, and how can I use them as running "scenery" in the sermon?
- Who will benefit from the truths in this text?
- What felt needs and real needs does this text address?
- What principles does this text teach?
- How have I experienced the truth of this text?
- What are the truth tensions related to this verse (for example, sovereignty and free will)?
- What is the purpose of this sermon?
- What is the cause, nature, and effect?
- How do I define the key words or ideas?

- How does this compare and contrast with related subjects?
- What does this text call us to do, say, think or stop doing, saying, thinking?
- What is the good news, the hopeful aspect, of this text?
- How would skeptics object to this verse and how can I answer them?
- What emotions are touched by this text?
- Have there been any stories in the news lately that relate to this subject?
- What key doctrines does this text teach?
- What assumptions of our culture does this text challenge?

The questions on a heuristic can overwhelm, so the idea is not to answer every question, but to find ones that trigger our generative thinking and that suit the week's text and sermon. Develop a short list of must-ask questions, and a longer list for variety. When you hear a speaker who approaches a sermon in a helpful way, write a question that would help you think about your sermons from the same angle.

One overlooked method for stimulating generative thinking is *conversation*. Talk with someone about your sermon, about what your Bible study has turned up, about your questions or possible approaches, about what they find interesting or puzzling or frustrating about the subject. Talking is easier than writing. It stimulates the mind, crystallizes thinking, and elicits input from others.

Finally, there is *outlining*. Outlining is a part of editorial thinking when we organize a pile of raw data, but it also contributes to generative thinking. When we know the direction we want a sermon to go, an outline channels our thinking in specific directions.

An outline is a form, and forms stimulate thought. For example, Peter Leschak writes:

> Limits — that is, form — challenge the mind, forcing creativity. Let's say I wish to express romantic love. I could write a sloppy, gushy love note, but my effort would be better spent if I wrote a love sonnet. As soon as I decide to produce a sonnet, I'm restricted to 14 lines, a specific rhyme scheme and meter. In the process of trying to fit my feelings and ideas into this form, I'll end up exploring avenues and notions that

would never have emerged from a simple, undemanding note.
. . . The more you limit yourself, the more you set yourself
free.[5]

You will need to experiment to find which of these five techniques works best for you. "Not all invention techniques work for all people," advises Timothy Perrin, "but every successful writer develops techniques to find out what he or she wants to say. The key is to relax. Don't try to 'write.' Just let the ideas come with no criticism. The time for deciding one idea is better than another comes later."[6]

DIVIDE AND CONQUER

There are two ways to write a sermon. One is to block out a day each week for preparation and write the sermon from beginning to end that day. We know beforehand what text we will use and have perhaps given it some previous thought, but sermon writing is essentially a one-day, one-draft affair.

The other way to write a sermon is in stages, blocking out several hours on different days, with strategic purposes for each stage. The whole process may take no longer than if we did it all in one day, but the sermons are often better.

Most acts of creation involve staging, the prototype being perhaps the Genesis creation account. A painter often begins with a rough-out stage, in which she pencils onto paper various perspectives of a potential picture. After selecting one, she draws geometric shapes onto the canvas to achieve proper proportion. She then paints broad strokes of background colors, followed by increasingly more detailed work on the subjects.

Similar stages are involved in creating a sermon. "Staging" sermon preparation takes advantage of several principles of enhancing creativity:

1. *Separate thinking.* Generative and evaluative thought don't cohabit, as mentioned above, and so planning stages for each allows both to have full expression.

2. *Significant pondering.* Getting fresh thoughts requires overcoming a major obstacle: over-familiarity. Harvard psychologist Ellen J. Langer and graduate student Alison I. Piper conducted a

series of experiments showing how familiarity breeds "mindlessness," or the unthinking use of categories.

In one study researchers gave students a rubber band and a piece of a dog's chew toy (composed of a rubber-like material). Researchers told thirty students what each item really was; they told ten students only that the items "might be" a dog's chew toy and rubber band, among other things.

During the experiment, the researcher pretended he needed an eraser. Four of the ten students who had been told "This could be a dog's chew toy," offered the toy as a possible eraser. Yet only one of thirty students who were told explicitly what the items were recognized that the chew toy could also be used as an eraser.

Apparently, the categories that the students were given hindered their ability to think creatively.[7]

Our familiarity with Scripture, with sermons we or others have preached on certain texts, and with books we have read, can lead to a similar "hardening of the categories." While a Scripture text may have a wealth of insights about any number of subjects, we tend to see it as we or others have in the past.

Taking off the blinders of familiarity takes time and tenacious thinking. "The best way to get a good idea," said Nobel prize-winning chemist Linus Pauling, "is to get a lot of ideas."

The drawback of one-day sermon preparation is limited time for mulling over a text and message. Unless the text and theme have already been selected, it just doesn't allow time for the unhurried reflection — while driving in the car, taking a shower, or doing other mindless tasks — that staged preparation does.

3. *The role of the subconscious.* After we have absorbed considerable data on a subject, putting the information out of our conscious mind for a period of time can lead to clearer thinking and fresh insights. Many suggest that our subconscious mind assimilates and percolates ideas while our conscious mind is occupied elsewhere. The Holy Spirit can then bring these ideas to consciousness in fresh ways.

"Big ideas come from the unconscious mind," says David Ogilvy in *Confessions of an Advertising Man.* "This is true in art, in science, and in advertising. Stuff your conscious mind with information; then unhook your rational thought process. You can help this process by going for a long walk, taking a hot bath. . . . Suddenly, if the telephone lines from your unconscious are open, a big idea swells up within you."[8]

Sherlock Holmes, the celebrated detective, used to stop in the middle of a case and take Watson to a concert. Although the practical-minded Watson was annoyed by this, the case always fell into place shortly afterward. Apparently author, Sir Arthur Conan Doyle, understood how creativity flourishes in the unconscious mind.

4. *More input, better output.* Several years ago, when the prolific Ray Bradbury was interviewed on PBS, Dick Cavett posed this question: "How do you produce such massive quantities of good stuff?" Bradbury replied, "The more you put into your head, the more you can get out."[9]

Staged preparation allows the time necessary to input more information. If we plan preaching calendars in advance, we can create files for a sermon or series and fill them with relevant material we come across in our reading. Many pastors recruit a team of volunteer researchers, inform them of the preaching plan, and ask them to clip or copy relevant material. When the final week comes for sermon preparation, we have a file stuffed with articles and illustrations, the raw material that makes for greater creativity.

5. *Hard work.* Myths about creativity abound. Denise Shekerjian, in *Uncommon Genius,* writes about one:

> To our eyes, these striking moments of creativity stand as magnificent monuments that appear so suddenly and with such impact, we assume a genius has been at work. The appeal of such an assumption is strong. It's far nicer to think in terms of a mighty hand stretching down from the heavens sowing genius in the land than it is to believe in the kind of tedious plodding that goes into the cultivation of a creative idea. It's far preferable to believe in thunderbolts than it is to have to face up to the mundane, trivial workaday world. It might come as a disappointment, then, to realize that behind any creative piece of work is a lot of earthbound effort.[10]

Sermons inspired by the creative breath of heaven also result from earthbound work, the more hours the better. While staged sermon preparation doesn't require allocating more time, it makes it possible to invest more study time if we choose. Adding extra study hours becomes even more feasible if we take quarterly or semiannual study retreats to research future messages.

6. *Intense concentration.* While some breakthroughs result from inactivity, as mentioned above, the bulk of creative ideas come from laser-beam mental focus.

"The truly inventive state of mind," writes Peter Leschak, "approaches the plane of consciousness you'd hope to attain if you were driving down an icy highway and skidded into the path of an oncoming truck . . . concentration is the key to creativity."[11]

This explains the saying "Necessity is the mother of invention." Necessity motivates — *forces* — us to concentrate whether we want to or not. Although painful, deadlines are a creative person's best friend.

Those working on a sermon ten days, or ten weeks, before it will be preached can have that deadline urgency. Staged preparation creates artificial necessity, a series of deadlines. Basic research will be finished, say, ten days before a sermon. A rough draft, five days before. The final draft, two days before.

Staged preparation benefits creativity by spreading out study among several days' peak energy periods, thus allowing for peak concentration over the entire sermon process, not just the first few hours. In unprepared one-day sermon writing, we may run out of energy by the time we reach the finishing stages of a sermon, thus preventing our putting the high-payoff finishing touches and artistic elements into the message.

7. *Fresh perspective.* The things we're exposed to between stages of sermon preparation can trigger a new vantage point on our subject.

If we take advantage of staged preparation, we may serendipitously see a picture in *National Geographic* or an article in the newspaper that provides a key metaphor. Or we may have a conversation that opens our eyes to a new relevance for the text.

How we stage sermon preparation depends on what works best for us. Here are two options:

Three-stage preparation: In the first stage, study the text and develop a sermon skeleton. In stage two, write the sermon in whatever your style: manuscript, expanded outline, or combination of the two. In stage three, evaluate the sermon for weaknesses, fill in the gaps, polish where needed, and spice the message with artistic elements.

Some preachers take a study retreat several times a year and do stage-one work on a number of sermons or a sermon series. Then they do stages two and three on two separate days sometime within the last ten days before preaching the message.

Five-stage preparation: Stage 1: Study the Scripture. Stage 2: Develop the skeleton. Stage 3: Write the introduction and conclusion. Stage 4: Write the body of the sermon. Stage 5: Evaluate, edit, fill in gaps, and spice the sermon with artistic elements.

GET THE RIGHT FRAME OF MIND

"I know quite certainly that I myself have no special talent," said Albert Einstein. "Curiosity, obsession, and dogged endurance, combined with self-criticism, have brought me to my ideas. Especially strong thinking powers ('brain muscles') I do not have, or only to a modest degree. Many have far more of those than I without producing anything surprising."[12]

As this quote suggests, the mind-set we bring to our task is as important as I.Q. or work habits. Five to thirty minutes spent preparing attitude and emotions — whether through prayer, meditation on Scripture, or thinking about the needs of the congregation or the purpose of our message make our minds a more fertile place for ideas to take root, germinate, and grow. A long walk, five minutes with our eyes closed in an easy chair, a cup of coffee — these pay off in hours of higher productivity.

Here are some of the states of mind that contribute to creativity:

A Sense of Mission. The key to taking a project from conception to completion is a sense of purpose. Having a clear focus and purpose is crucial to maintaining drive and concentration.

When we think only in terms of trying to have something to say, we will falter for ideas. When we think in terms of what we want the message to accomplish, how we want to help people, ideas will flow better.

Love for fresh expression. Creative people are "repetiphobic." The dread of repeating their own or someone else's thoughts compels them to energetically pursue what is new. Creative preachers love to say things in ways that keep people thinking, feeling, alert. And so the simple decision, *I'm going to say this in a fresh way,* is often the first step toward creativity.

Joy. Especially creative individuals find pleasure, joy, even at times a sense of play in creating. "I've had days where sermons come with all the speed and spontaneity of Chinese water torture," writes John Ortberg, pastor of Horizon Community Church in Diamond Bar, California. "I've also had days where they seem to write themselves. The most common variant for me is how relaxed and joyful I am when I sit down to write."[13]

Ideas come more easily when we enjoy generating and experimenting with ways of expressing them. The hardest time to come up with ideas is when we don't want to write a sermon. Reluctance shuts down the creative juices. Even when dealing with serious matters, the message flows more easily onto paper when it is "sweet in our mouth," as Ezekiel would say.

Curiosity and wonder. The most difficult thing in the world to do is to preach on something we're not interested in, on a text that doesn't challenge our interpretive powers, or on a holiday that seems to have been fully explored homiletically. This is why many pastors avoid familiar, "mountaintop" verses in favor of obscure passages or choose to preach expositorily through books that daunt them. One of the first steps in fresh thinking for a sermon is to think about what intrigues or mystifies us about a text.

Naturally, not all of these attitudes are required to write a good sermon. Some creative communicators do best when they are brooding about the awful state of the world. And given the human condition, some weeks we have to write a sermon with the mental readiness of a crab. But for most of us during most weeks, when we can successfully put ourselves in the right frame of mind, the sermons that result will be fresher and more engaging.

Creativity is rarely an accident. In one sense we can — almost — control the process. We can create a setting, enhance the climate, and follow the principles that foster creativity.

But in another sense, we can never control it. Creativity is elusive, mysterious, and for that we can be glad. That is what makes the creative process satisfying and exhilarating for us and appreciated by others. So honor the process — and pray for a miracle!

3

Introductions That Get Listeners

A good introduction arrests me. It handcuffs me and drags me before the sermon, where I stand and hear a Word that makes me both tremble and rejoice. When all is said and done, I walk away from such a sermon in thankful amazement, wondering, *How did* that *happen?*

The purpose of this chapter is to try to understand (at a safe distance) how the introduction gives the preacher a psychological warrant to take people into the sermon's custody.

The authority of a such an introduction defies a preacher's mastery. The speaker's personality, the occasion, the mood of the listeners — not to mention the mysterious brooding of the Holy Spirit over the preaching event — each adds dynamics that are not totally under our control.

That being said, most great introductions have several things in common. And it is not surprising that the same ingredients are found in gripping journalism. These classic, journalistic elements, once learned and practiced, improve our preaching considerably.

Commanding preachers can, of course, take great liberties with the "rules." Still, more times than not, the classic structure remains, for sharpshooter and beat-cop alike, an effective model.

STEP ONE: THE OPENING SENTENCE(S)

As we learned in elementary homiletics, an introduction must do two things: engage the listener and unveil the subject. What we don't necessarily learn in homiletics, and what we learned only after studying and practicing journalism, was how exactly an introduction can do that.

The better introductions take certain predictable steps on the way to the sermon. We've noticed at least three: the opening sentence, the development, and the transition.

Writers refer to the first few sentences as the lead. The lead is the most critical part of an article: if it fails to hook readers, they turn the page. Of necessity, journalists learn to write interesting leads. William Zinsser puts it this way: "The most important sentence in any article is the first one. If it doesn't induce the reader to proceed to the second sentence, your article is dead."[1]

The best sermon introductions also engage the listener immediately. Consider a few examples:

"When I was a boy growing up in New York City, one of the nicest ways for me to spend a Saturday afternoon was at the matinee of the neighborhood theater."[2] People love stories, and even a relatively tame opening like this immediately engages the listener: people want to know what happens next — and last.

"Have you ever asked God questions and felt you haven't received a good answer?"[3] Rather than building gradually to a difficulty people face, you can name it right off. Listeners identify immediately with a human problem they too have struggled with, and they are highly motivated to pay attention to discover a solution.

"Have you ever wondered why there is so much failure recorded in the Bible? It's obvious to even a casual reader of this book that its pages are strewn with the wreckage of men and women who have failed in their faith."[4] People love to solve puzzles. Mysteries beg for answers. Here the book that most of us think of as a compilation of the heroes of faith is described as a book of the failures of faith. People's natural curiosity will entice them to stay tuned until the puzzle is solved. Any sentence that points out incongruity, contradiction, paradox, or irony will do.

"Some years ago, the distinguished publishing house of Grosset & Dunlap brought together a panel of 28 educators and historians and asked them to select the hundred most significant events of history, then list those in order of importance."[5] People are intrigued by lists and by superlatives, as magazine cover copy at the supermarket counter proves ("Five Ways to Lose Weight," "Chicago's Top Ten Museums," etc.).

"I had never sensed such deep foreboding at the core of the Milky Way; I would have expected something friendlier and more chocolately."[6] An unusual comparison or metaphor piques the imagination, causing people to see something in a new way.

Each of these opening sentences comes at people from a different angle. But they all do the same thing: they arouse intellectual curiosity. They provoke listeners to want to know more. The opening sentence that makes people sit up and think, *Now that's interesting,* is the one to aim for.

When we try hard to be interesting, the temptation, of course, is to promise too much, or to say something shocking just to get people's attention.

One preacher began, "I want to tell you today exactly how to live your life and spend your money. I know I have your attention now . . . " Predictably, the sermon never told us "exactly" how to spend our lives and money. People will have patience with that trick for only a week or two, if that. They want us to engage them; they don't want us toying with them. When we promise something, we must pay up.

The opening sentence of a sermon is an opportunity. It's not crucial that we craft it perfectly — even the most apathetic will bear with us at least two or three sentences before turning us off. Still, it's a shame if we waste the moment when listeners are giving us their highest attention. If we do this sentence well, we won't still be working for people's attention when we are well into the sermon.

STEP TWO: DEVELOPMENT

Consider this example of a missed opportunity in development:
"It is a sobering, heart-rending scene. To have someone laugh at you — not with you, but at you — hurts, causes pain not unlike

that of a physical attack; indeed, ofttimes it is far worse. And yet, here it happens. The Son of God, Savior of the world, is the object of people's ridicule."[7]

Here the preacher identifies a common, unnerving human experience. However, before he invites us to recall a time in our own lives when others have laughed at us, or before he details a story about someone being laughed at with whom we can identify — hence, before we have a chance to *feel* the pain of that experience — he has jumped to the experience of Jesus. He merely stated the fact of ridicule; he didn't help listeners *experience* ridicule. He connected well with the head; he went too fast to get to the heart.

If the opening sentence aims at the listener's head, the development must aim at the heart. This is the most critical step in the introduction. Fail here, and we imply that we will be talking about a subject rather than speaking to living, breathing, feeling, needy people. Succeed here, and people will be unable to pull away from the sermon.

Thus, the second question to consider when crafting the introduction (the first is coming) is: *How can I reach the listener's heart?*

This is where most introductions fail: We aim primarily for the head, and we never engage the heart. When we fail to resonate with the listeners' interests and emotions, we've failed to connect with what most concerns people.

Note how this introduction from a popular news magazine approaches an abstract subject that few care about — the economy — through the doorway of what matters to them. Note how the writer intrigues the mind with the opening sentence and then engages the heart with the development:

> Robbie Aube is the kind of person sociologists like to say we need more of. For nearly six years he worked to build his construction business in Plum Island in northern Massachusetts. But the New England recession devastated the business, and his wife, Judy, sold few homes in her job as a real-estate agent. Aube, 38, analyzed their situation and realized drastic changes were needed. He took out a loan and went back to school for 18 months to retrain as an airplane mechanic. In a few weeks he, his wife and two children will move

to Minneapolis to take a job with Northwest Airlines. Did he agonize over the decision? "I said yes right there on the phone," he says. When times are bad, Americans have always picked up and tried to find prosperity somewhere else. This time, it may be tougher than ever.[8]

Most people in a recession ponder, with some trepidation, what it would be like to lose a job. This writer knows that the abstract issue of the economy is also a human issue, touching on basic human emotions like fear and anxiety and anger. Before jumping into facts and figures, he engages his readers by showing how the article is important to them.

It isn't necessary to fashion a full, dramatic scene to engage the heart. With the right choice of detail, a craftsman can capture both our interest and to some extent our feelings. Note the beginning of this sermon on Joseph:

> Joseph is the forgotten man of Christmas.
> He is Joseph the silent. In the Word of God, Joseph never says a word. He is talked to and talked about, but there is not a single syllable that comes from the mouth of Joseph, the adoptive father of Jesus. Joseph has the role of an extra. He is a character with minor credits. When we deal with our nativity scenes, he may be the last one set up and the first one toppled over. Even though there are fifteen cities in the United States named after him, Joseph is the forgotten man of Christmas.[9]

Although most people would be indifferent to the character of Joseph, within a minute, by the deft use of fact ("never says a word," "fifteen cities") and imaginative detail ("the role of an extra," "first one toppled over"), we begin to feel sorry for Joseph. That subconsciously touches our emotional need not to be forgotten.

These two examples show the development taking place within a paragraph, that is, in a minute or less. Normally, that is not a realistic goal — it is too much to try to accomplish in that short a time. Most good introductions take longer to develop. It takes time to engage the heart, but it is time well spent.

Note this masterpiece by Bruce Thielemann. He begins with humor and slight pathos. With that, he gently opens the door to our hearts. Then he steps in boldly and identifies a deep human fear:

It was on the wall of a subway in New York City. There was an advertising poster which depicted a dignified older gentleman recommending a particular product. And someone, probably a little boy, wanted to deface the advertisement, so he drew a balloon coming out of the mouth of this dignified older gentleman, and then this youngster wrote in the balloon the dirtiest thing he could think of. He wrote, "I like — ," and he meant to write "girls," only he made a mistake, and instead of writing "girls," he wrote "grils." "I like grils."

Then someone had come along and with a felt-tipped pen had written under that, "It's 'girls,' stupid, not 'grils.'"

Then another party, for the handwriting was still different, had come and written under that, "But then what about us grils?"

Now what about us grils? What about the people that nobody seems to like? What about the people who feel they've been crowded out of the middle of life, shoved aside, pushed somewhere they don't want to be? What about us grils?

A young man sat in my apartment about three weeks ago and with tears rolling down his face told me that the other kids thought he was weird. They oft-times isolated him. He told me in so many words he was a gril. Well, this sermon is dedicated to him.

A girl in her middle twenties said to me some months ago that she wanted to get into the middle of the garden of life. She wanted to be the kind of flower that people sometimes saw and noticed and appreciated. She was saying to me, in so many words, "I'm tired of being a gril." And this sermon is my response to her.

I know an older gentleman who deeply loved his wife and lost her to death. They were a beautiful couple in every way that you might choose to describe people. They were lovely to behold and deeply devoted to each other. When she was gone, he said to me with tears (grils cry a lot), "Life seems to be passing me by. It's rushing on all the time, and I don't seem to be able to get on to it anymore. I'm on the outside looking in, and it makes me desperately lonely." He was saying to me in so many words that he feels like a gril.

Then there's the person who's isolated because he's fat. They know people look at their fat and think about their fat. There are people who are homely. There are people who have never been taught the social graces. They feel awkward, as if they have three legs or four eyes. It's not a nice way to feel. It's like dying over a long, long time. It's hard being a gril.[10]

When Thielemann then announces that he is going to talk about a gril (Zacchaeus), anyone who feels like a gril (and that would include almost everyone by this point in the sermon) is arrested; they can't imagine at that moment anything more vital than to listen to the sermon.

WHAT ENGAGES PEOPLE

There is one overarching secret to getting people's attention at the beginning of the sermon: Talk about what people care about. Begin writing an introduction by asking, "*Will* my listeners care about this?" (Not, "Why *should* they care about this?")

The list of what interests people is nearly endless. Here are three examples.

• *Incongruity about deeply held beliefs.* For example: "Many people don't like the Old Testament, the First Testament as I am prone to call it. It is so full of wars and battles and dead bodies, and heads of dead bodies stacked like pyramids outside the city gates so that visitors are sure to get the message. There are floods and fires and fiery prophets who stare down kings and queens, and it really is good stuff — really better than *Star Trek*, better than *The Simpsons,* better even than the *Teenage Mutant Ninja Turtles* — but you can understand people's reluctance to read and study it."[11]

• *Things amazing.* An example from journalism:

With a modem, a telephone line and a bit of tail wind, the text of this story traveled from Galveston, Texas, to New York City in just over two minutes. It's an amazing feat made prosaic only by its regularity. But it's also yesterday's technology. The future apparently will be measured in *gigabits* — 1 billion bits of data, roughly a 20-volume encyclopedia — which can move across the land in barely a second. With that speed and accompanying power, scientists and schools, homes and hospitals could all be connected in one massive computer network. Then Everyman, and his sister, the physicist, will be able to dip into anything from the stacks of Harvard Yard to the video archives of the Home Shopping Network. All of that will be possible when the United States builds what has come to be known as a data highway, a fiber-optic spinal cord its proponents promise will do for the nation's economy and lifestyle what the interstate highway system did for America in the 1950s.[12]

• *The startling.* "Martin Luther was crazy, certifiably insane, hopelessly out of his mind."[13] Add to these a few others: a conflict, problem, tragedy, or pain; secrets, the unknown, the mysterious; something new, fresh; a story, whether true or a parable; a quote that is arresting or from a well-known person; humor; and of course, the big three: sex, money, or power.

It can never go without saying that what interests people most is God. He is the source of all good, all that calls to our deepest yearnings. This is why God is the subject of all preaching. But many people, even Christians, do not recognize their attraction to God, and sometimes we are wise to begin talking about God by talking about things people believe (falsely, of course) are nearest them: Their health and comfort. Their future. Their money. Their felt needs. Their problems. Their questions. Their parents. Their country. Their home. Their marriage. Their children. Their jobs. Their dreams and hopes. Their security. Their favorite books or TV shows or movies. And certainly, if we begin by talking about what keeps people awake at night, people will listen.

In addition, people are drawn to things weighty: a noble cause, great issues, people around the world. The common element here, however, is people. People care about people, and as a result they care about causes and issues and nameless humans on the other side of the globe.

The key, then, when dealing with an abstract subject — like the Trinity or eschatology — is to relate the subject to people, as did the journalist in writing the article on the economy. One television journalist associated with the highly popular *60 Minutes* says that the producers never do a story about an issue unless they can find a person to tie that issue to. They won't, for example, do a story about the rain forests being destroyed, but they would do a story about an individual's crusade against deforestation, or about how deforestation is affecting a particular family.

Many preachers, when stuck for an introduction, first think of a list of sources: what they have read (in books, newspapers, magazines) or watched (on television or in movies) or heard (on radio or in conversation) or experienced (in childhood, adolescence, and adult years) that relates to what they want to say.

Then they run those ideas through one question: Do people care about this? When you can finally answer yes, you've got the subject you can develop in the introduction.

STEP THREE: THE TRANSITION SENTENCE

The sermon introduction is sometimes described as a "hook." In that metaphor, the transition sentence is the last of the hook's three barbs, the first being the opening sentence and the second, the development. The transition sentence stirs further curiosity and interest by promising something: answers to the questions already raised, resolution of the complication, steps to be followed, principles that give insight. It is another of the journalist's tools used to propel the reader forward.

If the development is the most critical part of the introduction for the heart, the transition sentence is the most critical part for the mind. This is where we signal precisely what we are going to talk about for the next few minutes.

It can be helpful to think about this part of the sermon as a funnel between the opening development and what follows. As a funnel, it must be tight — one or two sentences at most. The longer it is, the foggier the thinking that underlies the sermon. The tighter it is, the clearer the thinking. Through these sentences all that comes before must funnel into what follows.

Thus the first and most critical question we ask in crafting an introduction is this: *What is my transition sentence going to say?*

In most cases, this is the theme sentence of the entire sermon. It tells people what the sermon is about. Note again the transition sentence in the article on the economy: "When times are bad, Americans have always picked up and tried to find prosperity somewhere else. *This time, it may be tougher than ever.*"

The author has just shown how one family has experienced tough times; now, albeit a bit more abstractly, he's going to talk about why many others may be experiencing the same thing for a while to come.

In the sermon about Joseph, after extending the development one more step, it says: "It could be said of Joseph that what he did speaks so loudly he did not have to say anything. Joseph is a remarkably simple person, and he is simply remarkable in his obedience to God."

By this two-sentence transition, the preacher promises several things. He promises to show us how Joseph's life speaks to ours today. He promises that the lessons from Joseph's life will apply to ours because Joseph was a simple person, a normal person, like most of us. He promises to show us remarkable (that is, surprising and interesting) things about how Joseph obeyed God.

If the sermon is the type that unravels its theme slowly, moving toward the conclusion through gentle twists and turns, like a great river, there still must be a transition sentence after the introduction, although the transition moves the sermon to only the next bend in the river.

In any case, because of their compactness, all transition sentences (here and elsewhere in the sermon) are the hardest sentences in the sermon to write. If they don't make sense both of what has gone on before and what is about to be said — and stir curiosity by promising something — they need more work. This is grinding but profitable labor, repaid by the continued attention and comprehension of the listener.

THE EFFECTIVE USE OF "WHITE SPACE"

Many preachers don't recognize that the introduction begins before a word comes out of their mouths. When they step into the pulpit, during that moment of silence before speaking, they already have an opportunity to engage people.

Silence is to sermons what space is to magazines. If an article simply begins in the upper left-hand corner of a page (or fails to use columns or uses all of the page for words), we're less likely to read it — it's just too intimidating. So at the top of articles, magazines not only use art, title, and deck to create atmosphere, they also effectively use white space. That white space gives the reader mental room to consider the article.

While pauses are powerful at any point in the sermon, a preacher can use the white space of silence especially effectively at the beginning of a sermon. Richard John Neuhaus writes of his experience waiting through the opening silence of the sermons of Martin Luther King, Jr.:

> During the times I was with Dr. King, I was struck by the way he did this almost consistently. Upon being introduced, or when the time came for the sermon, he would stand and wait, sometimes for ten seconds or more. It was what is known as a pregnant moment. It was a very active kind of waiting. His eyes would pass back and forth over the assembly, establishing his identity to them and theirs to him. Then, when all was quiet and it had been signaled that something important was about to happen, he would begin.[14]

Stepping into the pulpit calmly and scanning the congregation to the count of five can have a remarkable effect on preacher and congregation alike. It is as if you are saying, "I'm about to preach the Word of God. I want all of you settled. I'm not going to begin, in fact, until I have your complete attention."

Most of us will probably not get away with more than a five count, though. Preachers of the stature of Martin Luther King, Jr., can command more. If we were to try that, people would likely fidget, wondering if we had simply forgotten what we were going to say.

KEEPING THE INTRODUCTION IN PERSPECTIVE

As vital as the introduction is, a few realities can keep us from blowing out of proportion this part of the sermon.

• *Introductions can be too good.* We don't want to choose introductory material that is so intrinsically interesting that it entices people to mull over the introduction, thus falling behind the sermon.

An opening illustration, for example, about a tragedy — the death of an infant, the loss of a spouse, a loved-one getting AIDS — can make minds wander: *How horrible! How could that person handle it? What if that happened to me? How would I ever deal with it? I guess that's what happened to my friend, though, and . . .* Soon the listener is off in a land far, far way.

• *Introductions can't be too bad.* Introductions are a good deal like the Christian life. We are wise to craft them to be as engaging as possible. But when (not if) we blow it, we are wise to remember that grace covers a multitude of homiletic sins, and for a number of reasons:

First, we've got a captive audience. They are not going anywhere. And even if we bore them to aggravation, they will not get up and leave. We have a chance to redeem ourselves at any point in the sermon.

Second, church people are a generally polite bunch. They will do their best not to yawn or fidget or gaze off into space, and they will at least try to look interested in what we have to say.

Third, they are a humble group. They believe (mistakenly, I think) they know little about what makes for good preaching, so they often assume that if they're not tracking with their preacher, it is *their* fault! They feel it is their obligation as listeners to at least try to stay interested.

Fourth, people fade in and out of sermons all the time. In listening to sermons, we've all wandered out of one part, only to find ourselves engaged a few minutes later. If we don't hook people with the introduction, there's still a chance (although the odds are now worse) to engage them later.

In short, we preach by grace, both divine and human. We make our preaching a great deal easier if the introduction is well done, but we needn't despair if we see that the introduction didn't do the job we set out for it.

It's a rare sermon, however, that suffers because of a good introduction. A good introduction goes a long way toward arresting listeners, in the best sense of the metaphor. We want them to willingly, gladly, eagerly hear the good news that will follow, as if they had no choice. The well-crafted introduction is the best way of ensuring that.

4

Structuring Your Sermon for Maximum Effect

The human body, like the sermon, does many things at once: nerves transmit as the stomach churns as pores perspire as the heart pumps, pumps, pumps, pumps — many parts humming away, doing their separate work together.

The sermon, like the body, does many things at once, though this is not grasped by the novice. Our first attempts at preaching are desperate exercises in logic and clarity — all preaching boils down to constructing clear outlines. When that fails to bring revival, we embrace rhetoric; alliteration becomes all sufficient (and our congregations become long-suffering). When that likewise fails to spark Pentecost, we address felt needs — surely this is the key to effective preaching! And on it goes.

The sermon, though, is not a lock in need of a key. It is a living organism — not one thing, but many things, all humming away together.

Journalists want to communicate truth, but we soon realize that effective articles are more than words logically arranged. An article that is read — the only kind worth writing — must have clear writing about a fresh subject, but it must also touch the human heart, addressing some human concern. It must do at least these two things at once.

Though clarity goes a long way, it won't get us into the promised land of sermons that are listened to. In this chapter, we look at sermon structure: what are the various overarching elements that make the sermon, as a whole, work?

AN ANGLE

"No sermon is ready for preaching, not ready for writing out, until we can express its theme in a short, pregnant sentence as clear as crystal. I find the getting of that sentence is the hardest, the most exacting, and the most fruitful labor in my study."

This quotation of the eminent John Henry Jowett is a cliché in preaching circles, and for good reason: Jowett is right. A good sermon should drive home one thing, and if so, we can express it in one sentence.

As good as that advice is, it's not good enough. A sermon on "God" would concern only one thing, but that is too broad. Even "God's love" isn't narrow enough (we're not labeling files for storing sermon material). On the other hand, we can't preach on God's love for left-handed, bald wrestlers from Bolivia.

Here again, magazine journalism can help. An engaging article must be universal enough to appeal to a large number of readers and particular enough to say something interesting. When a writer discovers that combination, he or she has discovered the article angle.

We can often find the angle of an article in the subtitle, or "deck." Take a title and deck from the January 4, 1993, issue of *Newsweek:* "Something for Everybody: Clinton's cabinet is an exercise in diversity." The article is about President-elect Clinton selecting his cabinet. President-elects do that sort of thing, and only political junkies care.

But notice the angle the deck suggests: the cabinet displays unusual variety. This entices the reader into the article because it arouses two questions: Were my views or background represented in this group? Will this diverse cabinet work together in harmony and serve the best interests of the country?

The April 1993 issue of *Life* magazine ran the article "What Did We Lose?" with the deck, "Twenty-five years after their deaths, Martin Luther King Jr. and Robert F. Kennedy still make Americans dream." An article about King and Kennedy would be interesting, but the tighter angle chosen here — that their deaths still affect us today — is even more captivating.

In the same way, each sermon needs an angle, a topic universal enough to concern most listeners and particular enough to spark curiosity. Take, for example, Andy Stanley's sermon on "Conviction Versus Preference."[1] A sermon about living by one's convictions, though an important topic, lacks bite. So, Stanley pitted sticking to our convictions against living by mere preferences.

He might have taken other tacks, perhaps contrasting living by conviction with cowardice ("Convictions a Coward Can Live By") or sloth ("Taking the Trouble to Live by Convictions"). Or he could have preached about sticking to one's ideals ("Conviction in the Face of Compromise"). These angles invigorate an otherwise tedious topic.

Once we've determined this angle, every bit of sermon content should reinforce it. In the course of a sermon on conviction versus preference, one would not include illustrations of conviction versus sloth, or conviction in the work place.

Such consistency demands both courage and humility. The preacher's temptation is similar to the writer's: "Most nonfiction writers have a definitiveness complex," says William Zinsser. "They feel that their article must be the last word and the most comprehensive word. It's a commendable impulse, but there is no definitive article. . . . Decide what corner of your subject you are going to bite off, and be content to cover it well and stop. You can always come back another day and bite off another corner."[2]

A PURPOSE

Sermons need a purpose. The angle says what the sermon is about. The purpose says what the sermon should do, more particularly, what the listener will do as a result of the sermon.

Every sermon, by our definition, persuades. If it merely informs, let's say about the nature of the Trinity, we can call it teaching. Yes, yes, the line between *didache* and *kerygma* is blurry at points. But when the oratory primarily aims to sway listeners to do something religious — pray, love, worship, forgive, evangelize, trust, praise God — it becomes a sermon. (This is not to say that a sermon is an exercise in mere moralism: "Be patient!" "Be honest!" "Be loving!" Christian moralisms are always grounded in grace.)

Another question, then, to ask at critical junctures is "Does this section contribute directly to the sermon's purpose?"

The word *directly* is no accident. Preachers are notoriously indiscriminate in their choice of material — especially if it's guaranteed to draw a laugh. But if we're not fierce with ourselves at this point, the sermon will suffer, losing focus and force, perhaps confusing listeners as we try to do too many things at once.

A sermon that maintains a consistent angle and purpose will be clear, giving it a greater chance of being compelling. Still, a sermon, unlike a traffic sign, needs more than clarity.

RHETORICAL ROPES

A sermon on the love of God might have as its points:

1. The Pleasure of God's Love
2. The Purpose of God's Love
3. The Power of God's Love

This sermon's ultimate effectiveness, of course, would have nothing to do with those words that contain the letters *p* and *r*. Nonetheless, if we rope together a sermon with such a device, it pleases listeners. And pleased listeners listen better.

Created in the image of an orderly God, we're attracted to orderly things. Chaos unsettles us; order calms us. Randomness creates tension; order brings peace. One of the great themes of Scripture is that the confusion of this age will, in the age to come, give way to peace and order.

Though the other three aspects of the sermon — angle, purpose, and psychology — bring order, nothing so immediately communicates order to the listener as rhetorical ropes.

Alliteration is the easiest rhetorical rope to cast over the sermon, which is why it has become a cliché. Unless we handle alliteration subtly, without drawing undue attention to it, people will think it merely cute. We aim higher than that.

Fortunately, alliteration isn't the only rhetorical device that serves to structure a sermon. Here are a few more (though this is hardly an exhaustive list).

Clear, logical outline. This device, precisely because it is clean and rational, has high appeal. John Stott regularly employs it to good effect, as in this sermon entitled "Freedom":

Introduction: I've chosen to speak on freedom because:
1. Everybody is talking about it.
2. It's a great Christian word.
A. What we've been set free from:
1. Sin and guilt.
2. Self-centeredness.
B. What we've been set free for: to love God and others.
Conclusion: Give yourselves to Christ, and you will find freedom.[3]

Stott moves briskly through the sermon and at key junctures reminds us where he's been and where he's going. The listener could hardly get confused in a John Stott sermon.

The text. The standard rhetorical tie for expository preachers is the verses and phrases of a passage of Scripture. Though some congregations may find this pedantic, for others, especially those with a high view of the authority of Scripture, the structure of the text is structure enough for the sermon.

John Killinger exposits Psalm 46:10 ("Be still and know that I am God") in his sermon "The Nourishing Quiet." Laid out logically, the sermon would be

1. Take time for meditation and prayer.
2. Meditation and prayer help us know things with certainty.
3. Meditation and prayer help us know God.

That's clear enough, though unimaginative. Killinger likes to delight his listeners, so he hung the sermon directly on the framework of the text:

1. Be still.
2. Be still and know.
3. Be still and know that I am God.[4]

Or take Stuart Briscoe's sermon, "What About Shaky Marriages?" Since the points are manifold, the sermon risks becoming a disparate list. What holds it together is the text, 1 Corinthians 13:

      A. The greatest love is *Agape*.
      B. *Agape* accents behavior:
          1. It suffers long.
          2. It's kind.
          3. It's not jealous.
          4. It's not boastful.
          5. It's not proud.
          6. It's not rude.
          7. It's not self-seeking.
          8. It's not irritable.
          9. It does not keep a record of wrongs.
         10. It does not rejoice in evil.
         11. It rejoices in the truth.
         12. It always protects.
      C. How to develop *Agape*[5]

These points do not progress logically; that is, they do not follow a rational sequence. They are not the most essential aspects of love — for example, sacrifice and self-giving aren't directly mentioned. Moral theologians would probably structure the subject differently. But the sermon feels unified because its points arise directly from one text, and a familiar one at that.

An analogy. In his sermon "Life on Wings," Terry Fullam compares the Christian life to that of an eagle's:

1. You have to be born an eagle; you have to be born again to receive the gift of salvation.
2. Mother eagles shove babies out of the nest to get them to fly; God shoves us out into the world to mature us.
3. Eagles let themselves be lifted by the wind currents; we should let the Spirit lift us, strengthen us.
4. Eagles die while resolutely facing the sun; Christians can die with courage.[6]

The sermon doesn't have a centering text, nor does one point lead logically to the next. It simply reviews a few fundamentals of the faith. What holds the sermon together is Fullam's adept use of the analogy.

A warning to analogy makers: we've found it best to limit analogies to a few, salient, fresh comparisons. If Fullam had spawned comparisons — just as an eagle's claws grip branches, so should we grip the Word of God; just as feathers protect the eagle, so does the Spirit protect us — the sermon would have dragged.

Key word or phrase. A mere word or phrase, repeated at key junctures, can by itself structure a sermon. This is the stock and trade of African-American preaching. Richard John Neuhaus describes how one well-known African-American preacher employs this structure:

> Gardner Taylor begins by picking up a word, such as *reconciliation.* . . . First he just says it, but then you can see him warming up to it. Clearly he *loves* that word, and he's going to do wonderful things for it and to it. He tries just rolling it out of his mouth; then, staccato-like, he bounces it around a bit; then he starts to take it apart, piece by piece, and then put it together in different ways. And pretty soon you have a whole lot of people engaged in wondering and puzzling with Dr. Taylor, trying to figure out what this word and this idea of reconciliation is all about.[7]

Bruce Thielemann structures one of his sermons on one word, which, unsurprisingly, also serves as the sermon's title, "Because." He tells stories of sacrifice, of love, of faith, moving finally to God's forgiveness and love of us. At each juncture of the sermon, he asks "Why?" In each case he answers, "Because. Just because." All through the sermon, he demonstrates the truth of Pascal's dictum that the heart has its reasons that reason does not know.

Thielemann ends by quoting John 3:16 and then asking, "Why?"

We practically say the answer with him, "Because."[8]

Controlling metaphor. A variation on the key word or phrase is the controlling metaphor: when we refer regularly to some person, place, thing, or event that in some way visualizes the angle of the sermon. It's different from an analogy in that no series of comparisons are made.

For instance, Fred Craddock, in his sermon "When the Roll Is Called Down Here," uses a *list* as the controlling metaphor. He's preaching on the many names Paul mentions in Romans 16, but he makes the point that this isn't just a list; each person holds a special memory in Paul's heart. Craddock, through story especially, tells of important people in Paul's life and in his own life.

Then he tells listeners to make a list of people for whom they thank God. After a few moments, he says, "Have you written any names? Do you have a name or two? Keep the list. Keep the list, because to you it's not a list."[9] This non-list list, then, becomes a one-word metaphor for Christian community; it's a rhetorical device to hold together an otherwise disparate sermon.

Narrative. A narrative sermon, which tells an extended story, has a natural unity, as long as we follow the canons of good story telling.

Don McCullough ties together a sermon on "Gratitude" by personifying Gratitude and imagining him as his companion for two days. At the end of day one, he delights in the smell of baking cookies and the music of Bach when "Suddenly, I sensed a presence next to me on the sofa. He didn't speak, but somehow I knew . . . that his name was Gratitude. It felt right to have him there at the end of the day."

The next day, though, he forgets about his companion as he gets wrapped up in the day's activities, and especially when he learns of the death of a teenage girl of the congregation: "I don't know what happened to Gratitude in the next hour or so. I didn't kick him out of my office, but I sure didn't think about him."

That night, Gratitude lures him outdoors and shows him the stars littering the night sky. Gratitude says, "Visible only in the darkness." That's when McCullough realizes that Gratitude "was a friend for the darkness, too — a good companion, a very good companion."[10]

A PSYCHOLOGICAL CENTER

Finally, every sermon needs to have a psychological center. By "psychological center" I mean the fundamental emotion or need the sermon speaks to: fear, anger, gratitude, love.

Take Haddon Robinson's sermon "The Wisdom of Small Creatures."[11] The angle is not all that interesting: four fundamentals of faith. Robinson wants his listeners to rededicate themselves to these fundamentals. His points, stated abstractly, are

1. Read the Bible.
2. Trust in God.
3. Be part of a Christian community.
4. Don't despise fellow Christians.

The sermon, at this level of analysis, shows little sign of unity. It looks instead like a hodge-podge, the rookie preacher's four sermons in one.

But Robinson employs a series of analogies from his text to bring some external unity to the sermon. His text is the obscure Proverbs 30:24 – 28:

> Four things on earth are small,
>   yet they are extremely wise:
> Ants are creatures of little strength,
>   yet they store up their food in the summer;
> coneys are creatures of little power,
>   yet they make their home in the crags;
> locusts have no king,
>   yet they advance together in ranks;
> a lizard can be caught with the hand,
>   yet it is found in kings' palaces.

But just as important, the sermon is unified psychologically (effective sermons usually are structured and unified by more than one device). Throughout the sermon, Robinson highlights the vulnerability of each of these small creatures, showing how they compensate effectively for their frailties. He then makes an analogy with human experience.

For instance, just as ants must store food for winter, we can prepare for our winters (times when life is tough) — by reading Scripture.

Robinson then moves on to coneys, noting that they know how to avoid predators; they take shelter in mountain crags. Likewise, he reminds us where our security lies — in God. And so forth.

Since our vulnerability frightens us, we're drawn into the analogies, stories, and illustrations, which underscore the strength and safety we can have in God.

Yet Robinson never uses the abstract word *vulnerability,* and he never addresses the issue head on. He simply alludes to our fears and our yearnings by story and illustration. It is sometimes more effective not to directly mention the sermon's psychological center.

ALL TOGETHER NOW

At every juncture of the sermon, then, we can keep the various parts of a sermon working together for maximum impact by asking

- Does this contribute to the angle of this sermon?
- Does this contribute directly to the purpose?
- Is this consistent with the rhetorical ties?
- Does this contribute to the psychological center?

If the passage in question doesn't contribute, no matter how dear it is to us, no matter how much we crafted it, we must ruthlessly cut it. Annie Dillard, in *The Writing Life*, talks of this necessity in writing:

> A cab driver sang his songs to me, in New York. Some we sang together. He had turned the meter off; he drove around midtown, singing. One long song he sang twice; it was the only dull one. I said, You already sang that one; let's sing something else. And he said, "You don't know how long it took me to get that one together."
>
> How many books do we read from which the writer lacked courage to tie off the umbilical cord?[12]

We don't necessarily have to review paragraph by paragraph and literally ask these questions. But if we sense something amiss, if certain sections of the message just aren't working, these questions may point to the reason.

It has often been said that a sermon should be about one thing. To be more accurate, the perfect sermon has one angle, one purpose, one rhetorical tie, and one psychological center.

Perfection is rare, of course. Two out of four of the above elements will produce a pretty good sermon. Three out of four will produce a compelling sermon. When we're at our best, you see, the sermon does many things well, with many parts humming along, each doing its separate work together.

5

When You Can't Find an Illustration

You are fidgeting in your office chair on Saturday night, gripping your pen a bit tighter than usual, Bible and sermon notes spread out on the desk. You have developed a marble-solid outline for tomorrow's sermon, but the message lacks illustrations. It is as dense as a virgin pine forest.

It desperately needs the clearings, pacing, and breathing space that only an illustration can offer. You do a quick, nervous search through your memory's database but draw a blank. You finger through your illustration files but find nothing. What now?

As a pastor preaching three times a week for eleven years, I faced that dilemma often. But when I went to work for *Leadership* journal, I discovered that journalists — who live by the maxim: Illustrate more than explain — have ways of illustrating that had never occurred to me.

Some NFL quarterbacks enjoy the luxury of a full stable of thoroughbred receivers. The question is not whether the quarterback has someone to throw to, but to whom will he throw? Preachers with a full array of methods for illustrating a sermon enjoy a similar luxury. They don't worry about whether they will be "sacked," unable to illustrate an important idea. They have the freedom to choose between many types of illustrations, whichever one is open on the play and gives the longest gain.

Naturally, it takes some training to know and to adeptly use our illustrating options. Most of the great illustrators of our day — preachers like Stuart Briscoe and Steve Brown, for instance — say they work at illustrations. But the payoff at sermon time is effective communication — well worth the effort.

Our prime receivers for illustrating are

1. True stories
2. Fictional stories
3. Generic experiences
4. Images
5. Quotes
6. Facts

Furthermore, we can use each of these literally or figuratively, giving us all together twelve different ways to illustrate any idea. In addition to defining and illustrating each from a variety of sermons, we'll show how each type of illustration could be used to illuminate one particular theme, the need to persevere in prayer.

1. TRUE STORIES

Used Literally

True stories used literally are examples taken from life that illustrate the sermonic point directly. To illustrate courage, you describe a heroic act; to illustrate forgiveness, you tell about a time someone has forgiven another.

If we are illustrating the value of persevering prayer, for example, we could recount in some detail a story of a mother who prayed for years about her son, who finally, after decades of drug abuse and sexual license, became a Christian.

Maxie Dunnam, in his sermon "I Am the Door," tells a true story to illustrate how God answers anguished prayer:

> The most vivid experience of that anguished prayer and its answer that I can recall came in the life of a young couple. They were a bright young couple, handsome, with everything

going for them. They had the world in their hands. But then they played loosely with love, and she became pregnant before they were married. Without counseling with anyone, they decided to have an abortion.

Later they married, and everything went beautifully. They were successful in their vocations. Then they decided to have children. When I met them, she had been pregnant twice, but she had lost both the babies about eight or ten weeks after conception. And now she was devastated with anxiety because she was carrying the third child, and she was overcome with fear that she would lose that child also.

I will never forget the occasion when in torrents of tears, years of guilt poured out of her. It was guilt over that past sin, and fear — anguishing fear, a kind of hellish fear — that God was punishing her in the loss of those two previous children because of her past sin. And I will never forget, either, the restoration of their joy when out of that remorse and repentance they claimed the forgiveness of God in Jesus Christ. They renewed their commitment to him and allowed the door to be shut to that past.[1]

Used Figuratively

A true story used figuratively doesn't illustrate the point directly, but as an analogy. In order to make the connection between the illustration and the point, you have to make a transition, "Likewise . . . " or "In a similar way . . . "

To illustrate the value of persevering in prayer, we could tell a newspaper story of a man who proposed to a woman eight times over six years before she finally accepted. We might conclude, "In a similar way, prayer sometimes requires making repeated requests before it is answered."

In his sermon "How Do You Catch the Wind?" B. Clayton Bell begins the message like this:

> One Sunday morning a number of years ago my wife piled the children into the family car to come to Sunday school and worship. When she turned the switch to start, the engine wouldn't even grunt. The battery was completely dead.
>
> After lunch I went to a nearby service station and related my problem to the attendant. He went back to speak to the

station manager who was under a car on the grease rack. The attendant came back with this helpful offer. "Sure we can take care of it. Bring it on in."

Now isn't that the trouble with a lot of religion? You get instructions, but you don't get power. You get good advice, but you don't get the strength to carry it out. My friends, good advice without power is bad news.

That certainly is the dilemma of the Old Testament Law.[2]

2. FICTIONAL STORIES

Used Literally

If we can't find a true story to illustrate a point, we can craft one that directly corresponds to a homiletical point. Christ's parable of the Pharisee and the tax collector (Luke 18:9 – 14), for example, is a fictional story that corresponds literally to his point: don't trust in your own righteousness.

To illustrate persevering prayer in this way, we could create a parable of our own, a story of a woman who grew weary of praying day after day and in discouragement stopped. When she stands before Christ after her death, he tells her that he had intended to answer that prayer just before she gave in to her doubts.

Fictional stories used to illustrate what might have happened, as a foil to what actually happened, are particularly forceful. In his sermon "God Gives through People," about the story of Peter and John healing the lame man at the temple gate, John Maxwell says,

> Think about each one of us coming to church on Sunday, and somebody out front is begging from us, trying to stop us from going to church. I can think of things Peter and John didn't say — but boy, they sure could have said.
>
> For example, I can see them saying, "Well it would be nice to help you, fellow, but our service starts in five minutes, and we've got to go. We've got to pray. I mean we understand you have a need; the problem is you got us at the wrong time. You've got to have a need when we don't have other things scheduled."
>
> Or I can hear them saying something like this: "Well, look at all the other people going into the temple this morn-

ing. Let one of them help. I mean, there are hundreds of people going this morning. Am I the only person here who can help people? Do I have to do it all?"

Or I can hear them say something like this: "What a shame. What a terrible shame for a beggar to sit right outside our beautiful sanctuary. Boy, it just doesn't look right."[3]

And on Maxwell went, giving another three fictional incidents, each of which illustrated some aspect of selfishness.

Used Figuratively

When we use fiction figuratively, we're using a story as an analogy or an allegory. Nathan the prophet used a fictional story about a man and his lamb to rebuke David for his sin.

If we were illustrating persevering in prayer, we could make up a story about an ant, to whom we ascribe human thoughts and personality. Despite doubts and discouragement, this ant perseveringly drags a relatively huge piece of bread the full length of a driveway. "The ant's struggle with bread," we might conclude, "is like our struggle with prayer. . . . "

Here is an example from the "To Illustrate" column of *Leadership* journal:

Some scientists, according to a story by Harold Bredesen, decided to develop a fish that could live outside of water. So, selecting some healthy red herring, they bred and crossbred, hormoned and chromosomed until they produced a fish that could exist out of water.

But the project director wasn't satisfied. He suspected that though the fish had learned to live on dry land, it still had a secret desire for water.

"Re-educate it," he said. "Change its very desires."

So again they went to work, this time retraining even the strongest reflexes. The result? A fish that would rather die than get wet. Even humidity filled this new fish with dread.

The director, proud of his triumph, took the fish on tour. Well, quite accidentally, according to official reports, it happened — the fish fell into a lake. It sank to the bottom, eyes and gills clamped shut, afraid to move, lest it become wetter. And of course it dared not breathe; every instinct said no. Yet breathe it must.

So the fish drew a tentative gill-full. Its eyes bulged. It breathed again and flicked a fin. It breathed a third time and wriggled with delight. Then it darted away. The fish had discovered water.

And with that same wonder, men and women conditioned by a world that rejects God, discover him. For in him we live and move and have our being.[4]

As this illustration suggests, sometimes the best fictional stories are literally fantastic.

Fictional stories require extra work. A bare bones narrative will get a so-what response. Fictional stories need interesting, specific, imaginative detail about the persons and scene. They need dramatic features — dialogue, scenery, conflict. Furthermore, the better they employ irony, surprise, hyperbole, and understatement, the more persuasive they will be for listeners.

The benefit of fictional stories, though, is control: we can tailor them to our specific needs and tastes. Unlike true stories that we have to take as is, we can craft a fictional story, as Jesus did his parables, to have the characters say and do precisely what we need them to do and say.

3. GENERIC EXPERIENCES

Used Literally

A generic example describes a common human experience in general terms. Though it doesn't contain as many specifics as do stories, it still can stimulate our listeners' memories and feelings, helping them grasp a homiletical point.

A generic example used literally is one that corresponds directly to the sermon point. If we were illustrating persevering prayer in this way, we might say, "You pray night after night, month after month for a friend sick with cancer. You're worried for him and his family. You don't know what to say; some days you don't know how to pray. . . . "

In his sermon "I Am the Door," Maxie Dunman says,

You never really know a person until you know how that person perceives himself. I'm sure you have had experiences like I've had when you were sharing with another person, and that sharing became deep, when pretensions were dissolved and defenses failed and honesty prevailed. You sat on the edge of your seat, or you stood at attention in your mind to listen to what that person had to say, because you knew that person was sharing his innermost feelings about who he is and what he's about.

Those are the kinds of moments when people really meet, when deep calls unto deep and soul touches soul.[5]

As in this example, the subject of a generic example is often *you*, but we can also use *we*, or the third person: *a person, a Christian, Christians, hurting people.*

The literal generic example is especially useful during an application of a point. Jim Dethmer uses it in his sermon "The Gift of Mercy":

Is there a want-to in your heart? Is there something you want to do, but you are timid? Maybe you want to take a public stand for Christ. Maybe in the last couple of months you've trusted him as your Savior, and you know that baptism is coming up. You're looking with wide-eyed anticipation. You want to walk up on this stage or out into that lake and be baptized. You want to have your friends, your business associates, and your family, stand at the edge of the lake while you publicly proclaim Jesus Christ as your Savior and Lord, but you're fainthearted.[6]

Used Figuratively

Common, generalized experiences can also serve as analogies.

To illustrate persevering prayer, we could describe the experience of running to the mailbox each day for a long-awaited love letter, being disappointed again and again, but nevertheless running to the mailbox again the next day, until finally our letter comes. "The true spirit of persevering prayer is like that," we conclude.

Once I illustrated fear of the future with a generic, figurative example:

We all know the feeling of being afraid of the dark. As a child we would lie in bed at night and imagine a bogeyman under the bed, or a stranger in the closet. We would be too afraid to get up and go to the bathroom. If we heard the smallest sound, we knew that a dangerous murderer was pushing into one of the basement windows and would soon be coming up the stairs, knife in hand.

The same thing happens when we face an uncertain future. We lose a job or a relationship ends or health fails — suddenly the future is dark — and bogeymen and murderers threaten us.

Generic examples are easy to write. They draw in listeners, inviting them to put themselves into the experience. In terms of emotional impact, though, they are one step removed from stories. Also, where stories will entertain even if people don't identify, generic examples work only if the example is common to all. And if generic examples last too long or are used too often, they grow tiresome.

4. IMAGES

Used Literally

Unlike stories and experiences, the point of using images as illustrations is to give us a picture, not a plot.

Some mental snapshots are powerful: the marines raising the flag at Iwo Jima, John Kennedy slumping forward in his limousine in Dallas, Billy Graham with Bible open in one hand while his other hand slices the air. Such images convey emotion, carry deep meaning, even tell a story. When described with a direct application (e.g., the flag raising at Iwo Jima as an image of victory), the image is used literally.

To illustrate persevering prayer in this way, we could describe a childhood memory: "I'll never forget waking up early one morning and stumbling into my father's study. There he was on his knees, head bowed, face taut with intensity. He didn't even hear me enter, and he jumped when I tapped him on the shoulder. Over the years, I discovered, my father prayed like that nearly every morning."

In his sermon "Reasons To Be Thankful," an exposition of Psalm 138, Charles Swindoll explains,

> [David] says, "I will sing of it before the gods." . . . It's easy for us to forget that this little finger of land called Palestine was actually an island of monotheism surrounded by

a sea of polytheism — paganism, heathendom — whose idols were numerous, and often obscene. . . .

If you ever have the privilege of traveling in the Orient, you will see the gods visibly. You will see them on rooftops, and you will see them by door posts. You will see them stories high, covered with gold. You'll see their feet and legs as they sit like huge, fat giants, marked by blood and the droppings of candles. You'll smell the incense.[7]

Used Figuratively

Images used figuratively are essentially metaphors and similes.

If we were illustrating persevering prayer in this way, we could describe how a marsh is turned into usable land: trucks dump into the water rocks and dirt, most of which disappear from view. All the fill is necessary, but only the final loads seem to have an effect. We conclude, "All our prayers are also a part of the answer, although the first prayers seem to go for naught."

Jim Dethmer, in his sermon "The Gift of Mercy," says,

> The exhorter, the merciful person (is) like the rubber tires set up around a go-cart track. . . . When we get out of control, when we stray, we hit them and bounce back.
>
> James says that whoever turns a sinner from the error of his way will save him from death and cover a multitude of sins. The ministry of admonition, of warning, is the hardest of all the ministries of the encourager, the mercy-based person. It's a strategic ministry. Without it, the go-carts career off the track, through the parking lot, and out onto the highway, where death is sure.[8]

Dethmer doesn't narrate any events here. Rather he gives an extended analogy that figuratively — and visually — illustrates how one thing resembles another.

The advantage of this type of illustration, as always with metaphor, is that it stirs the imagination and calls up associated memories, ideas, and emotions. Just as mirrors make a room feel larger, metaphors expand an idea, working on multiple levels to give a deeper texture to the sermon.

Another advantage is the endless supply of possible analogies. We live in a visual, image-saturated culture. The more mental pictures we use, the more memorable, evocative, and understandable will be our sermons. Images, generally easier to come by than stories, are an untapped resource for many preachers.

5. QUOTATIONS

Used Literally

Especially if the saying is pithy or insightful, we love to hear quotations from books, conversations, hymns, bumper stickers, TV shows or commercials, magazine articles, and newspaper editorials. Good quotations illustrate feelings, attitudes, desires, worldviews, opinions, beliefs, values, ideals.

To illustrate persevering prayer in this way, we could quote, say, famous missionary Adonirum Judson: "I never prayed sincerely and earnestly for anything, but it came; at some time — no matter at how distant a day — somehow, in some shape — probably the last I should have devised — it came."

John Huffman, in a sermon titled "Meeting Your Family's Material Needs," used quotation to illustrate:

> There is no place for the lazy Christian. . . . I'm talking about your daily down-to-earth work routine.
> Fulton Rindge was a sage New England textile executive. He commented about a lazy associate, saying, "If Carl worked half as hard at doing something productive as he does at trying to avoid work, he would be a millionaire!" Some people are just plain lazy. Are you?[9]

Used Figuratively

A quote can serve as an analogy. To illustrate persevering prayer in this way, we could compare the need for persistence in prayer with the tenacity of American North Pole explorer Robert Peary, who said, "For twenty-four years, sleeping or awake, to place the Stars and Stripes on the Pole had been my dream."

Bruce Thielemann, in his sermon "Legions of the Unjazzed," uses a quote as an analogy:

> "There is a need in all of us," Phil Edwards says, "for controlled danger. That is, there is a need for activity that puts us on the edge of life. There are uncounted millions of people

right now who are going through life without any sort of real, vibrant kick. I call them the legions of the unjazzed."

Phil Edwards is not a theologian; he's not a philosopher; he is not given to writing; he's not a poet; he's not a lecturer or teacher. He happens to be one of the world's champion surfers. And he's writing here about surfboard riding. But as I read his article, and as I thought about him, I became more and more convinced that's what the Christian life is supposed to be like. I say this with all reverence: We are to be riding through life on a surfboard with God.[10]

Quotes are readily and alphabetically available in numerous quote books, as well as in daily life. Finding them can sometimes be time-consuming but is worth the effort. Good quotes are dramatic, often humorous, memorable, and interesting. They lend authority and pithiness to our ideas. When they reflect the opposite of what we believe, like a dramatic foil, they create tension and energy in the sermon.

6. FACTS

Used literally

Objective, verified data — such as demographic statistics, historical facts, scientific information, and the like — can simultaneously prove and illustrate.

To illustrate the need for persevering prayer in this way, we could tell about a survey that shows how few minutes the average Christian prays each day, concluding with, "It is clear, then, that we're not as persistent in prayer as we could be."

William Willimon, in his sermon "Don't Think for Yourself," illustrates with statistics the slide of values and morals in America:

The book *The Day America Told the Truth* says that 91 percent of us admit we lie routinely. Thirty-one percent of us who are married admit to having an extramarital affair lasting over a year. Eighty-six percent of youth lie regularly to their parents, and 75 percent lie regularly to their best friends. One in five loses his or her virginity before the age of 13. Two thousand two-hundred forty-five New Yorkers were murdered by their fellow citizens last year, an increase of 18 percent. Two-thirds of those asked about religion said it plays no role in shaping their opinions about sex.[11]

Used Figuratively

Spiritual and moral realities often resemble the physical realities that data describes, providing intriguing analogies.

To illustrate persevering prayer in this way, we could say, "Traveling at near the speed of light, electricity pulses through the room instantaneously — we flip the switch and immediately the lights go on. Sometimes, though, even moving at 186,000 miles per second seems slow. Traveling at that speed, it would still take us over four years to get to the next nearest sun in our galaxy. Likewise, some of our prayers to God will be answered instantly. Others addressed to the same God, will take what for us seems like a long, long time."

Calvin Miller, in his sermon "The Mind of a Servant," says,

> [The brain] operates at various levels of activity and frenzy. For instance, if the brain is operating at zero to three cycles per second, it is in a theta stage, a coma kind of a stage, and death is pending. If the brain speeds up to a delta-wave condition, four to six cycles per second, it is a deep sleep common to some sermon series on Leviticus. If it speeds up to between seven and thirteen cycles per second, it's in a beta stage, which is a creative, restful stage of man. If it speeds up to fourteen to twenty-one cycles per second, it's in the alpha stage, the typical Baptist stage that is perfect for baking casseroles and going to meetings. And at twenty-one plus, it is in a gamma stage, which is a hassled, hurried, frenzied state of life.[12]

If Miller had applied these facts figuratively, he could have said, "In a similar manner, our inner person has different stages of spiritual intensity."

This type of illustration is especially interesting to our information-oriented culture. Facts, though they may take a significant amount of research to unearth, bring an air of authority to a sermon.

Erasmus said we learn to communicate well by developing the ability to say something in a variety of ways. In one of his books, he took the sentence "Your letter has delighted me very much" and rewrote it 150 different ways by changing syntax and using synonyms.

A similar discipline with illustrations develops our ability to both see and use them. As an exercise, we could take a sermon idea and try to illustrate the same idea in each of the twelve ways described in this chapter. This would force us to illustrate in ways we rarely use, help us gain an eye for useful material, and develop our creativity and research skills.

"Between the amateur and the professional . . . ," said Bernard De Voto, "there is a difference not only in degree but in kind."

Preachers who deliberately broaden their illustrating skills improve themselves not only in degree but in kind. They think in ways they once did not. They see in ways they once could not. Like fine screens, the categories named in this chapter sift daily life, catching illustrations that once drifted by. We soon find that we can illustrate nearly any point, and gold nuggets now and again end up in the pan.

APPENDIX 1: A CHECKLIST OF SOURCES

One of the critical skills of a journalist is research, an academic word that simply means knowing where to find information and digging it out. Our culture is an incomparable mother lode of sources for illustrations.

Scripture
Personal experience
Newspapers, TV news, news magazines
Cartoons
Personal interviews
TV programs
Movies
Literature
Radio
Church history
Encyclopedias
Christian magazines
Secular magazines

Fiction
Biography
History
Art: pictures, sculpture, photography
Quotation books
Anecdote and illustration books
Printed sermons

6

Good Illustrations — and Great Ones

At any Fourth of July fireworks display, some rockets capture more attention than others. There are the delicate sprays that gently "puffph," sending to one side a dozen streaks of red or blue. There are the dazzling sky-fillers that radiate spokes of fire into a gigantic wheel of light. Then there are, what I called as a boy, the "boomers." Their launch sounded a bit louder. I would spot a small flash in the sky; a moment later the intestine-vibrating concussion thundered over the golf course; kids squealed with ear-aching delight.

Like fireworks on Independence Day, illustrations put light, color, and excitement into our sermons. They celebrate the sermon's ideas and principles. The small ones — allusions, analogies, and clever turns of phrase — are designed to support small points. But when we want to drive home the major theme, we had best send up our most powerful and illuminating illustration.

As a preacher and as editor of *Leadership*'s "To Illustrate" column, I have reviewed literally thousands of illustrations. I have noticed that the same elements that make for good journalistic writing make for good illustrations in preaching. Here are seven of the most powerful elements.

SPECIFIC RATHER THAN GENERAL

This is Journalism 101. "Use specifics" is a fundamental axiom of creative writing courses; it is fundamental because it is vitally important, and it is vitally important because it marks the difference between being interesting and being boring.

Being specific means saying *Luger,* rather than *weapon;* '89 *Taurus,* rather than *vehicle; adultery,* rather than *sin; the nails through Christ's palms,* rather than *Christ's sufferings; Bob, the 45-year-old, overweight Chicago detective with the scar on the back of his hand,* rather than *the officer.* The gunpowder is in specifics, the more precise the better.

Terry Fullam, in his sermon "Life on Wings," tells how mother eagles force their young to fly. If he had spoken in generalities, he would have said, "When their fledglings are old enough, eagles actually destroy their own nest to force the offspring to fly."

But Terry used specifics:

> The mother eagle stands on the edge of the nest and begins to pick up the feathers and the leaves from the lining and cast them over the edge. There they go.
>
> "Mother, what are you doing?" Mother eagle pays no attention. She takes out the interior of the nest. She takes the great sticks, and with her strong beak she snaps them in two. She turns them up on end — pulls the place apart.
>
> "Mom, what are you doing?" She pays no attention. She begins to disassemble the nest, and the branches go plummeting down the face of the cliff.
>
> "Mom, we're not old enough to go out into the world." But she doesn't pay any attention. Is she trying to break up housekeeping because she doesn't like her children any more? Not at all. She understands something they don't know. They weren't made to perch in the nest. They were made to soar, and they will never soar as long as they are in the nest.[1]

Three specifics have dramatically improved this illustration. First, Terry details the destruction of the nest, with branches being snapped in two, and feathers, leaves, and branches tumbling over the side. Second, he offers the thoughts of the young eagles. By articulating their fears and objections, we enter the story. Third, instead of *fly* Fullam uses *soar,* which communicates the nobility of the eagle's flight. One strategically specific word can make or break an illustration, turning a fluorescent light into a laser beam.

General words stir as much excitement as generic products. Specifics explode because listeners can better see, hear, feel, and experience the illustration. Specifics command attention, enticing listeners.

We tend to use generalities for compelling reasons. Specifics often take research and extra thought, precious commodities to a pastor. Generalities are safe; no one accosts us after church arguing that the nails were put through Christ's wrists not his palms, for example. We can't help but use generalities when we can't remember details of a story or when we want anonymity for someone. Still, the more specific their language, the better speakers communicate.

ABOUT PEOPLE RATHER THAN THINGS

"How can we put a face on this?" That's an editor's question. What he or she means is, How can we wrap this issue or problem around a specific person? Editors know that readers dive with interest into articles about people.

In his sermon "What about Shaky Marriages?" Stuart Briscoe says that men and women often cannot understand each other. He could have used computers to illustrate this: "Your IBM computer requires IBM-compatible software. If you try to run Apple software, on it, your IBM computer simply can't read the program."

That illustration would make the point, but it lacks the power of the illustration Briscoe actually used:

> Clint Eastwood made a movie called *Heartbreak Ridge.* . . . There is a side story in that movie where Eastwood — the 24-year-veteran marine gunnery sergeant, Congressional Medal of Honor winner — has lost his wife, who doesn't want anything to do with him. This big macho man is quite pathetic. He doesn't know what to do, so he starts buying women's magazines. You have a remarkable picture of Clint Eastwood reading women's magazines to find out what on earth his wife really wants. The tragedy is that it's perfectly obvious to everybody else, but not to Clint.[2]

This seizes our interest. The average church attender finds *People* magazine more engaging than *PC User*. Listeners identify with people's emotions, thoughts, opinions, appearances, problems, successes, strengths, and weaknesses. While illustrations drawn from nature, mechanics, or mathematics can help clarify, people illustrations are more likely to stir emotion. They are alive.

STORY RATHER THAN IMAGE

One of the biggest movements to hit journalism in the last twenty years has been the trend to use fiction techniques in nonfiction writing. In other words, use techniques of storytellers — plot, suspense, character development, metaphor, climax, dialogue, scenes — when reporting the news or telling Sunday readers how to fix the plumbing. Nothing is more interesting than a well-told story.

The importance of stories in sermons does not mean that images, which make abstract ideas concrete, are not crucial to good preaching. For example, in his Christmas sermon, "Glory to God in the Lowest," Bruce Thielemann says,

> We have an observatory in California called Mount Palomar, where there's a great telescope that can look out into space and pick out light so far away that it takes one hour of focusing upon that light for it to make even the faintest impression upon a photographic plate — tremendous capacities for focus in that telescope. But that is nothing compared to the way in which God focused himself in that baby. One little girl said Jesus was the best picture that God ever had took.[3]

While such images can be effective in sermons, when it's time to make a larger impact, a story works better.

Howard Hendricks tells this story:

> There's a running controversy in art circles as to who is the greater: Michelangelo, the pupil, or Bertoldo, the teacher. The great teacher Bertoldo knew gifted individuals are prone to ride rather than develop. He warned Michelangelo repeatedly, but with no effect.
>
> One morning he walked into the studio and watched Michelangelo as he was piddling on a little piece of statuary. Bertoldo went over and picked up a sledge hammer and batted

it into a thousand pieces that ricocheted all over that room. In the stunned silence, he shouted, "Michelangelo, talent is cheap; dedication is costly."[4]

Stories, even more than images, provide impact through their plot, conflict, climax, resolution — and their curiosity, human interest, life, surprise.

BOTH EMOTIONAL APPEAL AND LOGICAL APPEAL

In his sermon, "The Wisdom of Small Creatures," Haddon Robinson says,

> A while ago I was trying to fix our garage door. I came to that one screw I had to get loose, and the more I worked to loosen that screw, the tighter it seemed to get. A neighbor came over and saw my plight. He looked for a moment or two and said, "Oh, this has a left-handed thread. It's a reverse screw. You have to tighten or loosen it going in the opposite direction."
>
> It took me fifty years to find out how screws work, and now they change the rules! There's a sense in which all of the Bible is kind of a reverse screw. Everything in the culture that seems right, in the Bible comes out wrong. The way up is the way down.[5]

This story is effective emotionally and logically. We identify with Haddon's frustration over the stubborn screw and his surprise that a reverse screw exists. When he ties these common human emotions to a grand truth, the story is complete for us.

Less powerful would have been a merely logical illustration: "American League hitters struggle if and when they are traded to the National League. They've been accustomed to a higher strike zone, so for a while, they tend to get a lot of called strikes on low pitches, which they have trained themselves to lay off. It's the same way when you first read the Bible; God seems to change the rules. What was once a ball is now a strike, and vice versa."

Emotion alone can be as empty as cotton candy. Logic alone can be clinical, a tasteless meal of vitamin pills. Together, they are a full course meal.

TRUE RATHER THAN HYPOTHETICAL

One of the most gripping opening sentences in any newspaper article is something as basic as the dateline: "March 5, 1970, Boston, Massachusetts. Three south side residents . . . " A dateline is interesting because immediately you know that this is a true story, and truth is often stranger than fiction!

Again, in his sermon "The Wisdom of Small Creatures" from Proverbs 30:24 – 28, Haddon Robinson is describing the destructive power of locusts. He could have said, "Imagine a plague of locusts sweeping through the breadbasket of America, consuming all the wheat and corn standing in the fields. They would leave behind a natural disaster costing millions of dollars."

Instead he said, "What the locust and grasshopper cannot do alone, it can do in community with others. Back at the turn of the century there was a plague of locusts in the Plains of the United States. In the matter of a few days that swarm of locusts swept over the states of Nebraska, Iowa, and Kansas. In less than a week they did over five hundred million dollars worth of damage (in the currency of that time)."[6]

Robinson's true story rings with authority. It's interesting. While someone can argue or doubt a hypothetical situation, a true account "proves" its point.

SHOW RATHER THAN TELL

"Show versus tell" is another axiom out of Journalism 101. The amateur who taped the police beating of Rodney King in Los Angeles didn't need to say a word to add to the power of the scene. The power was in our seeing what actually happened.

Instead of standing between listeners and the story, *telling* people what to think, that is, interpreting and explaining a scene, a preacher can *show* listeners what happened and let listeners learn for themselves as they see and hear the scene through the description.

"Johnny was mad" is telling; "Johnny turned red, clenched his teeth, and pounded his fist on the table" is showing.

At the beginning of one sermon, a preacher told this story:

A few years ago, I had the opportunity to spend time with some well-known winners — professional athletes, best-selling authors, renowned business leaders, financial author-ities, televangelists, and even a few political leaders — winners, by anyone's definition. What surprised me about my interaction with many of these celebrated winners was that their victories had not seemed to satiate their desire to be win-ners. On the contrary, I came to understand that in many cases their victories had merely whetted their appetites to con-tinue to succeed no matter what the cost.[7]

This is better than no illustration at all, but it's a bunt single rather than a home run. Why? We never see the mannerisms and hear the words of these athletes for ourselves. We are forced to ac-cept the speaker's assessment of their lopsidedness.

The illustration would have grabbed us, though, if he had let us see one of those unsatisfied winners, perhaps, "I bumped into one guy who towered over me (his biceps were as big as my thighs), and we started talking. I asked the obvious: 'Are you in pro sports?'

'No more,' he said. 'But I played linebacker for the Pittsburgh Steelers a few years ago.'

For the next forty-five minutes I sat nodding my head and say-ing nothing. He talked about himself, his records, his big plays. And he proudly showed me his Super Bowl ring.

Finally, I interrupted him, 'So tell me about your family.'

'Well, to be honest,' he said, 'I'm separated from my wife, and she has custody of the kids.'

'That must be pretty tough.'

He glanced away. 'Yeah, sometimes it really bothers me,' he replied quietly. Then he looked me in the eye. 'But in order to win, you have to pay a price,' he said sternly. 'I worked long and hard to play in the Super Bowl. Nothing and no one can ever take that away.'"

For the listeners, the curtain is pulled back. *Showing* lets lis-teners gain insight for themselves. It raises curiosity and brings im-mediacy. If that jock spilled his drink, every person in the church would get wet.

DEVELOPED RATHER THAN ALLUDED TO

One preacher said, "Think of it. One maverick molecule running loose in this universe outside the sovereignty of God could be the very thing that disrupts every promise God has ever made to his people!"

He illustrated with this one-sentence allusion: "A grain of sand in the kidney of Oliver Cromwell changed the course of western civilization."

Allusions to stories have built-in limitations. First, ignorance: the majority of listeners would not know how Cromwell died. Listeners would understand the point but miss the emotional impact. Second, proportion: even if listeners do know a story, a glancing reference impacts less than a developed story, unless well-known allusions are piled up for cumulative affect, as in Hebrews 11. With an allusion, the listener's mind is like a flat stone skipping across the surface of a river and landing on the opposite shore; it gets wet but not submerged.

The more developed an illustration, the more its details are allowed time to sink in, the more a listener's senses and memories and emotions are engaged, the greater will be its effect. Listeners need to get interested and care about the people involved, all of which takes time.

Joel Gregory, in his sermon "He Cannot Be Hid," does more than briefly allude to Diocletian's unsuccessful attempts to stamp out the Gospel of Christ:

> In one wave after another that continued until A.D. 298, it looked as if Emperor Diocletian, the last persecuting emperor, was going to destroy the Christian faith from the earth. When you look at Eusebius's church history, you find they took Christians at Alexandria, North Africa, cut their tongues out, boiled them in oil, and threw them into the sea. In the Roman Coliseum, they threw Christians to the lions. Diocletian imprisoned the preachers, murdered the Christians, and took their books and burned them to ashes. In fact, he erected a column in the city of Rome, and on that column was written in Latin: *Extincta Nomina Christianorum.* It proclaimed in triumph the name of Christ extinct. But a strange thing happened. Diocletian divided his empire up, and the fel-

low who came after him in A.D. 312 looked up and said there at Milvian Bridge, "I see something strange in the sky." It was the cross of the Lord Jesus Christ, and next to it the words, "Under this sign, conquer." Whatever you think about Constantine and his conversion, I'll tell you this: Jesus cannot be hid.[8]

On the Fourth of July, the explosive celebrations across our land are not staged by amateurs. Professional pyrotechnic engineers, thoroughly trained and following strict safety guidelines, plan the show, design and pack the missiles, arrange and load the mortars, and finally light the fuses. Because these technicians can anticipate the patterns and effects of their gunpowdered art, we enjoy a fabulous show and, more important, celebrate a notable day in our nation's history.

Following these seven guidelines, preaching technicians will do no less.

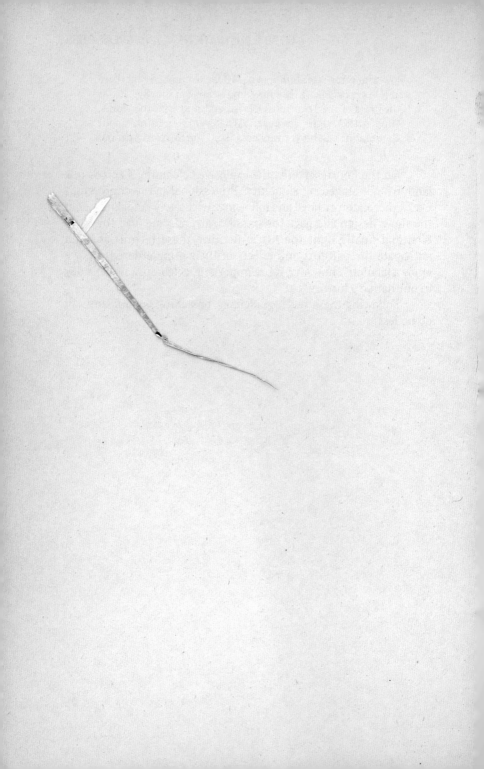

7

How to Tell a Good Story

Throughout his conquests, Alexander the Great read the *Iliad*, a book that kindles martial zeal. He often placed his copy, annotated by Aristotle, under his pillow at night alongside his dagger. It's not stretching it to say that this one story's effect on Alexander may have changed the course of history.

I confess I had been preaching for years before I realized well-told stories wielded this kind of power, that they could actually change people's lives. I happened onto that realization the hard way. My college degree was in accounting, and I've always felt at home with facts, analysis, and principles — the abstract and conceptual. I would have been embarrassed to simply tell a Bible story in a sermon — that was for children. I thought adults needed a quick summary of the story followed by cogent lessons from it.

But then I became pastor of an inner-city church in Chicago. I began to notice my sermons had less impact than in my previous location, a college town. I wasn't shirking on preparation. I painstakingly studied and outlined each text. But my people too often had blank looks. So I set a goal to learn how to communicate to my people, none of whom were college graduates, and a few of whom couldn't read.

Other inner-city pastors emphasized oratory and delivery, so I bought a book on classical rhetoric and tried becoming a flame thrower. Blank looks became surprised looks.

Then I read *Triumphs of the Imagination,* by Leland Ryken, which discusses the nature and value of fiction. Frankly, I hadn't read fiction in eight years. But Ryken argued that a story has power — in itself. Hearing one, we enter the experience of others, feel what they feel, learn firsthand.

So I tried recounting Bible stories in my sermons, accenting dialogue, building suspense. I began woodenly, then loosened up and found I actually enjoyed telling the stories! Best of all, my people now had looks of interest. They were enjoying the stories too.

Since then I've read many more books on storytelling and fiction writing. I've found that the same principles these yarn spinners use to make characters appealing and heighten suspense have aided my preaching.

CHARACTERIZATION

People love people. Many magazines exist solely because of this fact. We are inspired by other's accomplishments. We are curious about their secrets. We are attracted by their virtues and repelled by their flaws. For good or ill, we are never neutral about people.

Fiction writers know that, and they labor to create characters that will bond with the reader's interests. If we care about their characters, we will keep reading their book.

God has filled his Book with fascinating people: Joab, a no-holds-barred pragmatist; Abigail, an unflappable crisis manager; Jonadab, a crafty schemer; or Jonathan, the greatest friend anyone could have.

In order to spotlight characters in a Bible story or modern-day illustration, I must know them. Fiction writers spend days imagining their characters' habits, emotions, weaknesses, abilities, ambitions, and fears. As I prepare to tell a story, I take the time to ask myself: Were these people extroverted or introverted? What was their relationship to God? Were they assertive or passive, impetuous or controlled, can-do types or defeatists? This thinking takes time, because people are complex. But if I don't do it, I end up with cardboard figures that are indistinguishable and boring.

One way to bring biblical characters alive in my mind is to find contemporary parallels. Recently Jeroboam took off his sandals and put on black wing tips for me. Here is the consummate one-minute manager, high on the list of corporate headhunters. He is ousted from management only to return to claim the presidential suites. Yet he compromises principles and loses out with God.

Another way to ensure that the characters in my sermons are vital is to concentrate on the universal elements of their personalities: ambition, loss, romance, unfulfilled desires, success, stress, and so on. Some time ago when I preached an expository series through the life of David, I wrestled with the text where David feigns insanity. Then I spotted the common denominator — when facing a crisis, David was resourceful. The text sprang open.

I have also found that biblical characters are more relevant if I unveil their possible thoughts and motivations. My listeners know the complexity of their own inner lives. They identify with the character when they discover his or her personal struggles.

For example, I imagined Sarah's reaction when the Lord promised Abraham, "I will surely return to you about this time next year, and Sarah your wife will have a son," something like this:

"Sarah was speechless. Then came a sudden association, a memory sadly pushed to the back of her mind years ago: God had promised they would have offspring as numerous as the stars of the sky. She had never known what to think of that. And now, at this word from these strangers, she did think, *After I am worn out and my master is old, will I now have this pleasure?*"

It's easy to slide into the rut of characterizing by adjectives only. Though adjectives are useful, especially when time is short, fiction writers use many means to make each person in the story vivid and memorable.

- *Dialogue.* We get to know others by overhearing what they say.
- *Actions.* Play-by-play is perhaps the easiest way to inject life into a sermon.
- *Thoughts.* "As water reflects a face, so a man's heart reflects the man" (Prov. 27:19).
- *What other characters say.* One person brings the best out of our character; another the worst. Together they give the whole picture, like a statue viewed from different angles.

- *Description of appearance.* We discern much about others just by looking at them.

DIALOGUE

Of those methods for enlivening a character, dialogue is perhaps the most powerful. Some fiction writers advise that dialogue should make up one-third of the novel.

Among the most memorable words in the Bible are those from dialogue. What preacher would want to do without Moses' answer to God at the burning bush: "O Lord, please send someone else to do it"? Or Abraham's words to a curious Isaac as they climb a mountain of Moriah: "God himself will provide the lamb for the burnt offering, my son"?

I have found that using dialogue in my sermon stories helps in several ways.

First, dialogue invites immediacy. It beckons the listener to eavesdrop on each conversation. The storyteller gathers the listeners and the characters into the same room by using direct quotation rather than indirect. If I quote only indirectly, I put myself between the listeners and the scene: "Jesus then told Nicodemus that unless a man is born again. . . . " However, when I quote directly, I let the character do the talking: "I tell you the truth, unless a man is born again. . . . " A subtle change, but a noticeable improvement in immediacy.

Second, dialogue heightens emotion. Which has more drama, "Elijah sat down under the broom tree and felt depressed," or "Elijah sat down under the broom tree and said, 'I have had enough, Lord. Take my life; I am no better than my ancestors'"?

Third, dialogue reveals the person. We learn much about Naomi through these few words: "Don't call me Naomi. Call me Mara, because the Almighty has made my life very bitter. I went away full, but the Lord has brought me back empty." In a sermon I could say, "Naomi had been through great hardship and felt self-pity and bitterness," but her own words reflect that more powerfully.

Because my listeners intuitively gauge the character of a person from his or her words, I am particulary careful how I paraphrase and deliver the dialogue of biblical characters. Slang and regional accents can add humor and contemporaneity, but they can also mislead or distract when used indiscriminately.

ACTION AND PLOT

When we recount a Bible story in a message, we obviously do not write the plot, nor do we alter it. The same thing applies to illustrations from books, news events, or our own lives. But learning what makes for a good plot has attuned me to the crescendos and decrescendos of a story. I want to be like the pianist who interprets a song more sensitively because of his grasp of music theory and composition.

When I was a teenager, I bought a classical music album entitled *Fireworks,* a marrow-throbbing collection of zeniths from various pieces. We owned other classical music, but I got every last spark out of *Fireworks.* My tastes have matured; I now enjoy quiet and subtle movements as much as the grand finales.

My storytelling has followed a similar path. At first I told stories like one long finale, trumpet blaring from beginning to end. But I have grown more sensitive to downs and ups. Now I reserve the highest intensity for the story's climax.

The key to understanding a story's plot and where the climax falls is identifying the conflict. Whenever I prepare to tell a story, I consider: What problems is this person trying to solve? What adversity is there to overcome?

I had told the story of Isaac's birth many times before I recognized and developed one of the subsidiary conflicts: Would Sarah ever laugh again? Would her life ever take on joy? This problem isn't verbalized until the end of the story. At the birth of Isaac, Sarah says, "God has brought me laughter, and everyone who hears about this will laugh with me." I decided to tell Sarah's story, basing it on the problem of her lack of joy.

Since conflict sparks interest, I'll usually begin my telling of a story with it. Normally I don't launch the story with an eloquent description of a person, landscape, or background events; I unload that cargo as the plot progresses. With Sarah's story I had to establish from the start her lack of laughter, unstated in Genesis until the end. I imagined her reaction to someone else's celebration:

"A new mother giggles with her family and friends. Sarah smiled too, but she couldn't laugh; she hadn't really laughed in years. She was glad for the mother, but it was a hollow gladness and a Mona Lisa smile. Would Sarah ever laugh again?"

Sometimes, feeling pressure from the clock, I rush the beginning of the story to get to the climax and make my point. Taking time to establish the person's struggle is difficult for me, a get-to-the-point person. But by slighting the conflict, I defuse the climax, leaving myself with an emotional dud.

For example, the parting of the Red Sea is a moving climax, but only if you've been through Pharaoh's repeated refusals and the ominous charge of the Egyptian cavalry. So when I told the story during a series on Exodus, I didn't skip a single plague. The greater the struggles, the more powerful the victory.

SENSORY DESCRIPTION

The doorways into the imagination are the five senses. By appealing to the senses, the storyteller takes listeners by the hand and leads them across the threshold into the scene. Notice how the following sensory-filled introduction involves you in Joseph's experience:

"Joseph's head pounded as he looked at the crowd of buyers and wondered, Which one will be my master? He wanted to get off his feet, blistered by the desert trek. As raucous, foreign tongues filled his ears, he longed for the voice of Jacob."

During my sermon preparation I close my eyes, place myself in the scene, and use my imagination. What do I see? What do I hear? What do I touch, smell, taste? When I put myself into Elijah's place at the ravine of Kerith where he was fed by ravens, the brook didn't just run dry. Stones hurt the back of my cupped hands as I pressed them into the river bed for the trickling water. In the message I won't use all these perceptions, just enough to satisfy a healthy imagination.

Of the five senses, sight is the most influential. Storytellers are like film makers searching for meaningful, emotive images: David twirling his sling, Abraham lifting a knife over his son, Adam hiding in the bushes from God.

Lengthy descriptions slow a story, so whenever possible I embroider description into the action. For instance, instead of saying, "Goliath's sword was heavy," I would say, "David strained to raise Goliath's sword over his head."

When we taste, touch, smell, observe, and listen, we tell the story freshly even to those who have heard the story ninety-nine times before.

DELIVERY

Rushing a story is like gulping down a Sunday dinner. It takes time to set the mood, to expressively speak the dialogue. Our listeners will not get emotionally involved in thirty seconds, nor can we build suspense in that time. We need pauses . . . silence.

There are occasions to speak rapidly, to increase the sense of fast action. But in general, a hurried story says, "Just get the facts." A slower pace says, "Feel this; live this." I used to balk at spending a large amount of time on a story, because I wanted to get to the point. Now I realize the story gets the point across better than my declarative statements.

By trial and error I have developed a storytelling style that works for me. I write out the story in my own words, then read as little as possible, because when eye contact is broken, the mood evaporates. And I tell a story without pausing for principles or application. I want people to experience the story itself in a powerful way first.

Telling a story well requires extra preparation, and when a story is long or I don't manage time well during the week, I read more during the sermon. I have faced those dreaded moments in which I am a few feet from the pulpit, with solid eye contact, and can't remember what's next. But those blunders are forgotten when a story hits home.

SURPRISES

As I increased the amount of storytelling in my preaching, I found I did not have to jettison principles and propositions. Instead of the traditional format of ideas, then illustrations, I first tell the story or paint the image, proceeding from known to unknown, concrete to abstract. This gives the listener a solid box for storing wispy principles.

Recently I preached on how we often push God to the side during the week and live for our own pursuits. But I began by telling of King Ahaz, who was charmed by a pagan altar in Damascus and carved a copy in Jerusalem. He took the liberty of moving the furniture in God's house, sliding his new altar into the center and the bronze altar to the side. Ahaz instructed the priests to sacrifice on his altar; at God's altar he would seek divine guidance.

Only then did I raise the question, "Aren't we like Ahaz if we devote time, energy, and thoughts to personal ambitions but seek God only when we can't pay the bills?" Weeks later a member confessed, "Pastor, that story showed me exactly what I was doing."

A second surprise from my increased story telling is that Bible stories have become my main resource for illustrations. The Bible is packed with stories — adventures, mysteries, romances. It has heroes, villains, suspense.

Through these stories, biblical events and characters become for listeners symbols by which they interpret their lives. A woman in my congregation once told me, "I used to complain a lot: 'Why do I have to go shopping today?' 'I hate to clean the bathroom.' But when you preached on the desert wanderings, and I saw the Israelites grumbling all the time, I just couldn't complain any more. And if I catch myself complaining, it hurts me inside because I don't want to be like them."

As I tell stories, I am affected as deeply as the listeners. Some time ago I sat with my boys at bedtime reading the story of David and Goliath from a children's book. I came to David's famous line: "All those gathered here will know that it is not by sword or spear that the Lord saves; for the battle is the Lord's, and he will give all of you into our hands."

For the rest of the story I fought back tears . . . just from reading a children's book.

I'm not given to tears, but pastoring in Chicago at the time, toe to toe with Goliath, I identified deeply with David. Suddenly, I was ready to fight again.

8

A Forceful Style

Words are chess pieces in the preacher's game. With them we aim to hold listeners' attention in check. The preacher, of course, plays white.

P – K4	P – K4

Standard opening struggle for control of the center.

KN – KB3 . . .

White attacks Black's pawn.

. . . KN – QB3

Pawn defended.

P – Q4 . . .

Pawn attacked again.

. . . P – Q3

Pawn defended again.

And on it goes. The preacher moves to get and keep attention, to get the congregation to take the Word seriously. The human mind being the complex, wonderful, unruly thing it is, checking attention is a complex, wonderful, and sometimes unruly task. At every move, the minds of parishioners counter with subtle parries:

Defense: *Why did he say that? What does he mean?*

Counter attacks: *What makes him such an authority?* or *I know this, tell me something new.*

Harassing moves to the flank: *I wish this service was over; I have a lawn to mow.*

Or, *I wonder if I'm going to be able to keep my job during this recession.*

Or, *I don't know what I'm going to do with my Debra.*

When the preacher develops pieces well, the congregation finally is cornered: their attention is riveted upon God, upon gospel — checkmate!

The only means of accomplishing this feat, or of even getting close, is to move deftly those chess pieces of communication: words.

We must move those words with purpose, with precision, in coordination with other words. Sometimes the words must be moved slowly, sometimes boldly and decisively. If we develop sloppily or too cautiously or attack prematurely — if we don't use words and sentences well — we will fail to get the congregation to think about the one thing they've gathered to think about.

Words and sentences are a large part of preaching. Annie Dillard, in *The Writing Life,* tells this anecdote:

> A well-known writer got collared by a university student who asked, "Do you think I could be a writer?"
>
> "Well," the writer said, "I don't know. . . . Do you like sentences?"
>
> The writer could see the student's amazement. Sentences? Do I like sentences? I am twenty years old and do I like sentences? If he had liked sentences, of course, he could begin.[1]

The more we like sentences, like to craft them, play with them for best effect, the more our people will like our preaching.

We are wise, then, to remind ourselves now and then of the fundamentals of word use. Naturally, manuscript preachers have more use for such rules. But we've noticed that many of the best non-manuscript preachers still write their introductions, conclusions, transitions, and key passages, especially when they need conceptual precision or want a certain emotional effect.

Again, journalists have much to teach us here. Words on paper are easily critiqued, analyzed, and edited, so print communicators have developed a wealth of maxims for how to best employ them. What's more, writers are grizzled veterans of the war for people's attention and understanding; they know how to use words.

Most of the following rules come from writers' manuals. We've found, happily, that they work for preachers too. No rule here, by itself, will make or break a sermon, of course. But a consistent breaking of these rules has a cumulative, weakening effect. Sentences, paragraphs, or the sermon as a whole, end up in stalemate. Attention to ten rules can prevent that.

1. OMIT NEEDLESS WORDS

"Vigorous writing is concise. A sentence should contain no unnecessary words, a paragraph no unnecessary sentences, for the same reason that a drawing should have no unnecessary lines and a machine no unnecessary parts. This requires not that the writer make all his sentences short, or that he avoid all detail and treat his subjects only in outline, but that every word tell."[2]

Such is the advice, sound and compelling, of William Strunk and E. B. White in their famous *Elements of Style*. What makes for good writing makes for good preaching.

Needless words weaken our offense. Listening to some speakers, you have to sift hundreds of gallons of water to get one speck of gold. With others, if you miss even one word or sentence, you've suffered a loss.

There are few sermons that could not stand some trimming of needless words and phrases. Here are a few of the more common places that can be done.

Cumbersome constructions. Some words don't add anything to a sentence. Find and eliminate them. For example, let's look at this quote from a published sermon:

"The relentless creativity of God has affected my life in such a consistent manner that I'd like to share with you what I'm learning."

Of God can be replaced with *God's* — genitive phrases can often be changed to possessive.

My life is a euphemism for *me*.

In such a consistent manner is a long way of saying *consistently* — prepositional phrases can at times be converted to a single adverb.

I'd like to share with you is pointless because, in fact, that is just what the preacher is doing.

The shortened version looks like this: "God's relentless creativity has affected me consistently; here's what I've learned." Twenty-four words down to eleven. Such tightening gives listeners the feeling that everything we say counts; they don't have to wade through filler for the payoff.

Red herring verbs. Many preachers introduce illustrations from their past with the useless phrase *I remember:* "I remember how when I was a small boy, I would cry at the sound of thunder."

This construction makes the preacher's *remembering* the principle activity of the sentence. Listeners are not interested *that* the preacher remembers, only in *what* the preacher remembers.

We might simply say, "When I was a boy, I cried when I heard thunder."

Participles. Participles often add needless syllables and words to sentences. For instance: "What Matthew is doing here is helping us see Jesus' freedom." Here *What Matthew is doing* adds nothing but syllables to the sentence; *is helping* can be shortened as well: "Here Matthew helps us see Jesus' freedom." (Beginning a sentence with the word *What* tends to create clunky sentences.)

Repeated words. Unless the emphasis is deliberate, you don't want to use the same word twice in a sentence: "The genealogy in Matthew is a carefully constructed genealogy." Better: "The genealogy in Matthew is carefully constructed."

Telling people what you're going to tell them. "I'm going to tell you something that happens here and probably all across the country at this season of the year." Don't tell people that you're going to tell them something. Just tell them: "It happens here and probably all across the country at this season of the year . . . "

Another example: "The first principle I want to discuss is give with a generous heart." Of course you want to discuss it. Better: "First, give with a generous heart."

This tendency also occurs when we're about to quote: "There was a verse written about three hundred years ago by an Oxford student. It says . . . " Better: "About three hundred years ago, an Oxford student wrote . . . "

Or, "Listen to this quote from William Shakespeare." Of course people are going to listen. Of course it's a quote. Better: "William Shakespeare wrote . . . "

Vague adverbs. Ironically, the word *very* dilutes the force of a word. "They stopped very abruptly" is less abrupt than "They stopped abruptly." Better still, say it clipped with a pause afterward: "They stopped."

Or what does *very* add to these sentences?

"Peter was a very diligent apostle."

"Jesus was very compassionate."

"The passage is very powerful."

Very usually doesn't add much. Neither do *highly, truly, quite, rather,* and *really,* among others.

Redundancy. If one word or phrase in a sentence does the work of another, it's redundant. "My friend has written one of the classic books on preaching that's in the literature of the field today." *Books,* by definition, are *literature; a* book *on preaching* can be nothing but *literature of the field; a classic* is usually something referred to *today.*

Better: "My friend has written a classic book on preaching."

There is, there are. We can usually tighten sentences that begin this way with no loss in meaning, rhythm, or emphasis: "There are three principles we can draw from this passage." Better: "We can draw three principles from this passage." The same rule applies to the past tense, *there were* and *there was,* and to sentences beginning with *it is* or *it was.*

One preacher began four out of five paragraphs like this:

"It was Jesus who challenged people . . .

"It's amazing how a thin piece of paper, two-and-a-half inches by six, can be so powerful. . . .

"Isn't it amazing how the dollar bill creates tension in the congregation? . . .

"It's not merely a private power we deal with today."

At least three of these become more vigorous and interesting by eliminating *it is* or *it was*: "Jesus challenged people. . . . The dollar bill makes congregations tense. . . . We don't deal with a merely private power today. . . . "

Verbal punctuation. In spoken language, we often employ verbal punctuation, words and phrases that signal breaks in the sermon:

"Now, we need to remember that when Jesus . . . " This use of *now* is useless in written English, but in a sermon it can signal the beginning of a paragraph.

And often acts as a comma or period. *Well* often acts like a comma or an exclamation point that precedes the clause to be emphasized: "Paul was, well, a Pharisee of the Pharisees." *By the way* works like parentheses: "By the way, when Paul uses the word *righteousness.* . . . "

The caution here is don't be careless. In the right place, verbal punctuation helps the sermon. Overused, it weighs the sermon down.

2. USE ACTIVE CONSTRUCTIONS

In baseball, intentional walks draw yawns. In football, prevent defense is boring. In novels, characters who get pushed around by forces beyond their control become tedious. In most settings, passive is dull. That's especially true in communication.

Passive verbs passify. Active verbs invigorate. When a sentence uses active verbs, fewer prepositions and forms of the verb *to be* clutter the scene; more importantly, the subject and action are clear. Unless we have good reasons to use a passive construction (perhaps we don't want to indicate who initiated the action), we should avoid it. "Jesus was struck by the high priest." Better: "The high priest struck Jesus."

"Peter and John were called by Jesus to follow." Better: "Jesus called Peter and John to follow."

Like action movies, action sentences hold attention.

3. BE SPECIFIC

A prosaic preacher might have begun, "The streets were crowded that morning in Jerusalem, filled with children, parents, and the aged, as well as merchants selling their wares."

But Peter Marshall began his sermon "Were You There?" like this:

> The morning sun had been up for some hours over the city of David. Already pilgrims and visitors pouring in through the gates. . . . There were the aged, stooped with years, muttering to themselves as they pushed through the throngs, and there were children playing in the streets, calling to each other in shrill voices. There were men and women too, carrying burdens, baskets of vegetables, casks of wine, water bags. And there were tradesmen with their tools. And there, under a narrow canopy, a merchant shouted his wares in a pavement stall.[3]

Marshall's introduction is more memorable and intriguing. Why? He used specifics: "stooped in years, muttering to themselves," "calling to each other in shrill voices," "carrying burdens, baskets of vegetables, casks of wine, water bags."

Specific words create pictures in listeners' minds, making for easier listening and better remembering. And whether we are attempting a descriptive scene or a simple statement, specifics add interest:

"Americans are consumed with materialism." Better: "Americans pant for wide-screen color televisions, Sony CD players, ski trips to Vale, and hot-red Miattas."

4. KEEP PARALLELISM PARALLEL

> There is a time for everything, and a season for every activity under heaven:
> a time to be born and a time to die,
> a time to plant and a time to uproot.
> Sometimes people go about killing, other times they give themselves to healing,
> Tearing down — sometimes tearing down old ideas, sometimes literally tearing down buildings — is something we do at certain times, and at other times we build up.

Thank God the author of Ecclesiastes knew the value of uninterrupted parallelism. But some of us, in the desire to make ourselves precisely clear, dissipate the power of our thought. In the following quote, if the preacher had not succumbed to the temptation to explain — "about the quality of your education" — his point would have been stronger:

> "Our world cares more about bombs for the enemy than about bread for the hungry. This world is still more concerned about the color of skin than it is about the content of character — a world more finicky about what's on the outside of your head than about the quality of your education or what's inside your head.[4]

5. AVOID JARGON

For preachers, jargon comes in two forms.

First, preachers are tempted to speak excessively in "the language of Zion," using biblical terms and theological language that the biblically illiterate cannot comprehend.

For example, speaking of the image of Jesus sitting at the right hand of God, one preacher said,

> The image implies . . . that Jesus is King. The one who alone was Priest and Victim, offering the sacrifice for all people and for all time, is now the King who rules the cosmos. The universe is in his care. His lordship is for all and over all. The derelict, forsaken man hanging in disgrace upon a cross on a hill outside Jerusalem is both sin-bearer and king-ruler. Who we see Jesus to be for us on the cross is also who God chooses to be through the Son in God's eternal rulership over the cosmos. *God always is for us.* That is what Christ's kingly rule at the right hand of the Father means.[5]

This preacher tries to explain one biblical image (Jesus sitting at the right hand) with a tidal wave of other biblical images (priest, victim, King, sin-bearer, king-ruler) and abstract language (God's eternal rulership over the cosmos, God is always for us). In the end, his jargon clouds rather than illumines.

Biblical images are powerful, so powerful that to explain them with other biblical images merely clutters the sermon. Instead, we want to use clear, simple, contemporary language.

The second temptation is to use abstract language. Abstraction is the business of scholars, especially in fields we preachers admire:

philosophy and theology. We're tempted to use abstractions when we want to sound learned. The problem is, when it comes to communication, abstractions usually obscure meaning. Even the best of preachers fall into this trap:

"One can hardly help being struck by the incredible flatness and secularity of existence in our time. Technology and the good life have apparently conspired to eliminate the quality of depth from the human consciousness."[6]

Though concise (a strength of abstract language), his language requires a great deal of concentration to understand. Most listeners won't get it.

Note a later sermon of the same preacher, though, in which the same general idea is made without abstractions:

"Entertained any mystery lately? Probably not.

"Our age isn't much into mystery. Oh, we dabble in it now and then — some Edgar Cayce stories, the Shirley MacLaine books, a little New Age philosophy. But for the most part we're a stockbroker, major airlines, GNP, no nonsense kind of society. We're trying to take the mystery *out* of life, not put it in — you know, solve the problems of a fluctuating economy, determine which brands to buy, eliminate the guesswork from medicine."[7]

6. AVOID CLICHÉS

A cliché is a phrase so commonplace that it is predictable. If we say, "We're all trying to keep up with — " people mentally add "the Jones" before we can say it.

If we say, "He was at the end of — " people mentally add "his rope."

Use too many such clichés, and listeners tune out. They think us unoriginal, boring, not worth listening to. And we won't be.

7. EXPRESS IDEAS POSITIVELY

The word *not* often clutters a sentence:

"He did not believe that daily Bible study was a necessary activity." Better: "He believed daily Bible study was unnecessary."

"Paul did not have much confidence in Mark." Better: "Paul distrusted Mark."

"Barnabas did not pay attention to Paul." Better: "Barnabas ignored Paul."

It is neither always possible nor desirable to eliminate the word *not*. When we can, though, it makes for bolder sentences.

8. USE SHORT WORDS

Beware of words that end with *-ness, -tion, -ization, -ful, -tive, -ious, -ence, -ance*. Such words often signal passive construction as well as abstraction.

"Mothers are the means to the continuation of creation." Better: "Mothers continue creation."

"He planned a banquet of pure perfection." Better: "He planned a perfect banquet."

"For Jesus, it was an inconvenience to attend to the woman." Better: "The woman annoyed Jesus."

"Herod was cruel in his governance of Judah." Better: "Herod governed cruelly."

9. SAVE THE BEST FOR THE LAST, OR THE FIRST

Mean
 is what he was:
  Knock me down;
  Rub my nose in the dirt;
  Say bad things about my pappy . . .
  things I knew weren't true
  and there wasn't a blessed thing I could do.
   That's one of the things that never changes.
   Sometimes when things go wrong
   there's not a blessed thing you can do.[8]

Here James Lowry, in speaking about a boy from his childhood, shows clearly the value of beginning and/or ending phrases with significant words. *Mean, knock me down, rub my nose, say bad things* have a cumulative effect, especially when Lowry changes his cadence by placing his key thought at the end of the next few clauses.

The beginning and end of clauses and sentences are prime real estate; that's where we want to place our most important words. Otherwise, sentences begin weakly or trail off, losing punch and momentum.

"You look up at the wall and see pictures of children and grandchildren, but they are all distant *to you.*" Better: ". . . but to you they are all *distant.*"

"If a vulture wants to attack a rock badger, it has to knock down a mountain *to get at it.*" Better: "If a vulture wants to attack a rock badger, it first has to *knock down a mountain.*"

Distant and *mountain,* since they are more evocative than *to you* and *to get at it,* will linger in people's minds.

A repeated emphasis on the beginning or the end can produce a strong effect, as in Haddon Robinson's "The Wisdom of Small Creatures" (quoted here in clause form to highlight the construction):

> Usually when we model, we model upwards.
> We place before us those men and women of God who have blazed
>   a path to glory —
> the heroes of the faith who have not only touched their times but
>   influenced the course of history.
> Agur, on the other hand, models down.
> He chooses four creatures that are small,
> and though he doesn't say it, they are not particularly appealing.
> There aren't many people who have pet ants.
> Not many people take coneys out for a walk on a leash.
> Find a locust or a lizard in your home, and you usually try to
>   stomp it to death.
> Yet Agur chooses these simple creatures, small and unattractive,
> and he models down, he gives us wisdom for the living of our days.[9]

Note how the last words of each clause intensify Robinson's points: *Upwards, glory, and course of history* — grand, noble words — end the first clauses; *small, not . . . appealing, pet ants, walk on a leash, stomp it to death, simple creatures* — ignoble ideas — end the second set of clauses. These last clauses are a nice contrast to his last words: *wisdom for the living of our days.*

10. AVOID SEXISM

1. Everyone has his own way of writing a sermon.
2. Everyone has her own way of writing a sermon.
3. Everyone has his or her own way of writing a sermon.
4. Everyone has one's own way of writing a sermon.
5. Everyone has their own way of writing a sermon.
6. People have their own ways of writing sermons.
7. Everyone writes sermons differently.

These are seven solutions to a contemporary problem: how to speak about a generic individual without assuming the individual is male. This is enough of a concern for enough of our people that we are wise to figure out a way to deal with it. Some listeners stumble if we consistently use masculine pronouns to refer to generic individuals.

Like each stylistic suggestion in this chapter, no particular instance will make or break a sermon. But a steady inattentiveness to this matter will give our sermons a tone that will undercut their effectiveness for many people.

Each of the above solutions has its merits and its problems.

1. *He*. The merit: it's traditional, and for many listeners it "sounds" right. The disadvantage: for many listeners it always assumes a male individual.

2. *She*. Some communicators alternate between male and female pronouns: the first generic example is a male, the next a female. This has the merit of variety, of including both sexes in the sermon. The disadvantage: it can startle listeners, drawing attention to itself, to the fact that you're being inclusive — and that's a distraction.

3. *He or she*. This solution has the advantage of including both sexes, and the disadvantage of making the sentence sound clunky. It is usually best avoided, but sometimes it cannot be helped.

4. *One*. This solution removes all sexual reference, but *one* makes the generic individual even more abstract, formal, and stiff.

5. *Their*. This solution also removes sexual reference, and without analysis sounds right, especially in spoken language. But given the current standards of grammar, it is incorrect since a plural

pronoun is being used with a singular noun. (*Harper's Dictionary of Contemporary Usage,* 1985, makes a strong case for using *they, them,* and *their* as indefinite singular pronouns, but this argument has yet to win the day.)

6. *People.* Often the entire sentence can be cast in the plural, which solves the problem at one level. But in this and many other cases, it undermines the content. Here we want to emphasize the individual — that's the point of the sentence.

7. *Active construction.* In some cases, the sentence can be entirely recast, avoiding the problem altogether — unless you need the cadence of the longer sentence.

In sum, no single solution to this problem can be applied to every situation.

BREAK THE RULES FOR GOOD REASON

Every rule mentioned here can be broken with impunity, depending on what you are trying to accomplish. Break the rules when the positive effect you will achieve outweighs the drag of clutter. Here are three examples.

We said that we should omit needless words. But in some cases, words that are needless for content are needed for rhythm. Strunk and White have noted this in analyzing a famous line of Thomas Paine: "These are the times that try men's souls." It's not hard to shorten it:

Times like these try men's souls.
These are trying times for men's souls.
Soulwise, these are trying times.
These are trying times.[10]

The shorter it gets, the worse it gets. Sometimes "needless" words are needful.

Or take the injunction to use active rather than passive verbs. Again, it depends on what you are trying to communicate. If you're trying to emphasize that Theresa is depressed, that she feels like events are just happening to her, you might write:

"Theresa was taken to the train station by a taxi. She was seated by a porter. Theresa found herself next to a woman, and a conversation floated between them for most of the trip. Soon Theresa found herself in London." You could recast each sentence in active, forceful verbs, but then it wouldn't *feel* as depressing.

One final example: Sometimes a seemingly awkward negative construction actually provides a nuance to a sentence and adds a touch of wry humor. It's one thing to say, "Peter was the worst person for the job." It's another to say, "Peter was unqualified for the job." It's another still to say, "Peter was not the worst person for the job." The first is harsh, the second, matter of fact. The third suggests Peter is unqualified, but does so with a smile.

No rule, then, is absolute; like a chessmaster deviating from the standard chess opening to pursue a well-planned line of attack, we can break each stylistic rule to great effect. But like the chessmasters, we have to know what we're doing and why, or sooner or later we lose our advantage. Even the masters of English stick to fundamentals; for them exceptions are indeed exceptions.

9

Crafting Words That Inspire

Why would a serious and sincere communicator, someone who long ago outgrew the callow urge to impress listeners with cleverness, use artistic elements like understatement, hyperbole, periphrasis, simile, repetition, parallelism, irony, even wordplay?

Here's why. Note the difference between the next two sentences, the first in plain prose, the second using artistic elements:

> Washington is not an efficient, charming city.
> Washington is a city of southern efficiency and northern charm. — John F. Kennedy

Plain speech is just that — plain. Artistic speech is interesting, dramatic, fresh, appealing, powerful. It fires the imagination. It speaks to the heart. It reaches corners of the human spirit that plain, literal speech misses. (Brain researchers say artistic speech speaks the language of a side of the brain that prosaic speech cannot reach.)

While the strength of literal speech is clarity, the strength of artistic speech is depth, the possibility of communicating on more than one level, of resonating with more of the soul than any Webster's-accurate prose can ever achieve. Artistic speech carries a bigger payload. No wonder it is used by the best contemporary communicators in speech or in print. It was certainly used by Jesus.

"Let your speech always be with grace, seasoned as it were with salt," Paul wrote to the Colossians. Though he was talking about conversation with unbelievers, his advice aptly describes the value of artistic, interesting preaching. People want to hear what we have to say.

This chapter isn't about "purple prose." Even if listeners responded to that, and contemporary listeners generally do not, few pastors have the time to do any more than salt their messages with artistic elements, primarily at the strategic points: the introduction, key sentences and paragraphs, and conclusion.

This chapter gives a recipe — nine ingredients — for salting a message with just enough artistic flavor to interest listeners.

COMPARISON

Comparison, or the use of metaphors and similes, is probably the most common form of artistic speech and offers the most imaginative potential. Scripture is full of examples: "The Lord is my rock, my fortress, and my deliverer" (Ps. 18:2).

A metaphor says one thing *is* another: "I am the bread of life." A simile says one thing resembles another, using *like* or *as*: "As the deer pants for streams of water, so my soul pants after God" (Ps. 42:1).

Comparisons are powerful because they are visual. Word pictures enliven the imagination and stir emotions. At a practical level, images keep the interest of today's visually-oriented listeners.

Metaphors can enliven an already dramatic scene and help the preacher talk about abstract topics in tangible ways that impact listeners.

In his sermon "Tide Riding," Bruce Thielemann accomplishes both these effects in this short passage:

> My first pastorate was in McKeesport, Pennsylvania, which was famous at that time for having the world's largest steel-tube rolling mills. . . . Many was the time I stood in one of those great machines . . . with the man operating the machine. I'd see a great serpent of molten metal come slithering down into the machine, and it would be chopped off. Then the machine would grab it by its end and begin to spin. By cen-

trifugal force, that bar of metal would open from the inside out. . . . Many times I asked the men directing those machines, "What's the most important ingredient in the process?"

The answer was always the same: "It's the temperature of the metal. If it is too hot, it will fly apart; if it is too cold, it will not open as it ought. Unless you catch the molten moment, you cannot make the perfect tube."

Unless we catch those molten moments when character can develop, we miss our opportunities just as the disciples did. . . . I do not know what would constitute a molten moment for you.[1]

Thielemann heightens our interest in the steel mill by introducing the snake metaphor, then uses "molten moments" as a tangible way to talk about the abstract concept *opportunity*.

Metaphor and simile set a tone. They can add drama, for example, as in Thielemann's snake metaphor, or humor, as in the following line from a Walter Wangerin sermon:

"The poor fellow's eyes were wide as boiled eggs, and he leaped up from the side of the ledge and started running."[2]

When we select a comparison from the world of our listeners, they identify with us: "People were lined up to see Jesus like 747s waiting to take off from O'Hare."

Metaphor and simile benefit from listener's thought associations, calling forth emotions, attitudes, and memories. In his sermon "Living a Life of Integrity," George Munzing says, "Integrity is not revealed when you are on stage, before the footlights of popularity."[3] The stage image calls forth the excitement people recall as they have given or received applause.

It is easy to misuse comparisons, and the fallout is serious. If the speaker makes too many of the following mistakes, the listeners suffer confusion or doubt the speaker's intelligence.

Mixed metaphor. Multiple images in close proximity confuse rather than enlighten, making a speaker look somewhat ridiculous:

"She charged into my office like a bull and fired one rocket of criticism after another. Finally she slipped into four-wheel drive and ran out of my office."

We are most prone to mix metaphors when using "dead" metaphors (those used so commonly that we no longer recognize them as metaphors): "If you can't take the heat, start firing back."

Overreaching. We reach too far when a comparison is illogical, weak, or nonexistent, or when we stretch the imagination too far: "Love is the tree sap of human relations. It nourishes the leaves of our soul."

The genius of great writers is their ability to use outlandish metaphors effectively. Pulitzer prize winner Annie Dillard brilliantly compares Christian worship and polar exploration, for example, in her essay, "An Expedition to the Pole." But without the genius's touch, extravagant comparisons sound silly.

Adverse associations. "The gospel is as powerful as a nuclear bomb." Though both things are powerful, the simile fails because it compares something fearful — nuclear holocaust — with something glorious — the good news.

"Joy is as infectious as the bubonic plague."

"The devil prowls the streets like Mother Teresa looking for the weak and dying."

Overuse. Continually talking about one thing in terms of another grows tiresome, because it forces listeners to keep decoding the comparisons.

CONTRAST

Contrast accentuates and intensifies, just as a match which is unnoticeable in the sunlight burns brightly in a deep cave.

Contrast makes for an appealing balance: "He is infinite God and I am finite man."[4]

"Instead of a hard-edged portrait, we get painting on velvet."[5]

Contrast is a staple of persuasive ethical and moral preaching. Bruce Thielemann, in the conclusion of his sermon "Tide Riding," says:

> Please don't say anything to me about tomorrow. Tomorrow is the word the Bible does not know. If you can find me any place in the Scriptures where the Holy Spirit of God says tomorrow, I will step down from this pulpit and never step into it or any other pulpit for as long as I live.

The Holy Spirit's word is the word today. "Now is the accepted time; now is the day of salvation." "Today, if you will harden not your heart and hear my voice. . . . "

Don't say tomorrow. "Tomorrow and tomorrow and tomorrow creeps in this petty pace and lights fools the way to dusty death."

The word is today. Come to Christ today. Grow in Christ today. Serve in the name and in the spirit of Christ today.[6]

Christ used contrast to underline the difference between past and present, between his teaching and other teaching: "You have heard that it was said, 'Do not commit adultery.' But I tell you that anyone who looks at a woman lustfully has already committed adultery with her in his heart" (Matt. 5:27 – 28). "You have heard that it was said, 'Eye for eye, and tooth for tooth.' But I tell you, Do not resist an evil person" (Matt. 5:38 – 39). Thus contrast is well-suited for contrasting truth with error.

Some of the most effective epigrams are merely clever contrasts: "War talk by men who have been in a war is always interesting; whereas moon talk by a poet who has not been in the moon is likely to be dull" — Mark Twain.

When contrast is overused, listeners feel like a spectator sitting too close to the net at a tennis match. The back and forth gets tiresome. As with all elements of artistic speech, moderation is the rule.

PARALLELISM

Parallel words, phrases, clauses, and sentences make our thoughts appealing. Parallel structure is a memorable way to show the relationship between abstract ideas:

"Sow a thought, reap an act. Sow an act, reap a habit. Sow a habit, reap a character. Sow a character, reap a destiny."[7]

"In the presence of God, he had a good eye on himself, a bad eye on his neighbor, and no eye on God."[8]

"Never in the field of human conflict was so much owed by so many to so few" — Winston Churchill.

Parallelism is memorable.

People would not decorate their bedroom walls with the Beatitudes if Christ had said, "Blessed are the poor in spirit, for theirs is the kingdom of heaven. Mourners will be comforted, so they're blessed as well. The meek, who will inherit the earth, are blessed. God will bless those who hunger and thirst for righteousness by filling them full."

Parallel structure highlights special nuances and distinctions of thought: "That comfort is not a knowledge that everything will be all right, but a knowledge that everything is under control."[9]

When a speaker piles up sentences and phrases in parallel structure, a tremendous sense of drama and emotion builds:

> We shall not flag or fail. We shall go on to the end. We shall fight in France, we shall fight on the seas and oceans, we shall fight with growing confidence and growing strength in the air, we shall defend our island, whatever the cost may be, we shall fight on the beaches, we shall fight on the landing grounds, we shall fight in the fields and in the streets, we shall fight in the hills; we shall never surrender.[10]

REPETITION AND REFRAIN

Repetition and refrain are another way to bring power to a sermon. Jesus not only used it in such passages as the Beatitudes (Blessed are the . . . , for they shall . . .) but also when he chastised:

> "Woe to you teachers of the law and Pharisees, you hypocrites! You shut the kingdom of heaven in men's faces. . . . "
>
> "Woe to you teachers of the law and Pharisees, you hypocrites! You travel over land and sea to win a single convert. . . . "
>
> "Woe to you teachers of the law and Pharisees, you hypocrites! You clean the outside of the cup and dish, but inside they are full of greed and self-indulgence." (Matt. 23:13ff.)

Or take a modern example, Martin Luther King's speech, "I Have a Dream":

> Even though we face the difficulties of today and tomorrow, I still have a dream. It is a dream deeply rooted in the American dream. I have a dream that one day this nation will

rise up and live out the true meaning of its creed: "We hold these truths to be self-evident that all men are created equal."

I have a dream that one day on the red hills of Georgia the sons of former slaves and the sons of former slave owners will be able to sit down together at the table of brotherhood. . . . I have a dream that my four little children will one day live in a nation where they will not be judged by the color of their skin but by the content of their character. I have a dream today.

I have a dream that one day. . . little black boys and black girls will be able to join hands with little white boys and white girls as sisters and brothers.

I have a dream today.

I have a dream that one day every valley shall be exalted, every hill and mountain shall be made low, the rough places will be made plain and the crooked places will be made straight, and the glory of the Lord shall be revealed, and all flesh shall see it together.[11]

This is one of the most dramatic speeches of the twentieth century, and the wave upon wave of "I have a dream" has embedded itself in the national consciousness.

Using an inherently dramatic artistic element such as repetition when the subject or setting does not warrant only backfires. Don't try it without passion. It will feel as awkward as wearing a tuxedo to a small group Bible study. It will fall flat, even striking some as a parody.

HYPERBOLE AND UNDERSTATEMENT

King Saul has just defeated the Amalekites. He and his troops are returning from battle, giddy over triumph, with sheep and cattle, fat calves and lambs plundered from the enemy.

The king, while exultant, also feels guilty. All this booty is a problem, for God had commanded total destruction. Saul catches sight of the prophet Samuel approaching. Feeling like a schoolboy with a croaking frog in his coat pocket, Saul puts on a Sunday-school smile and takes the initiative: "The Lord bless you! I have carried out the Lord's instructions."

Samuel isn't smiling. "What then is this bleating of sheep in my ears?" replies Samuel. "What is this lowing of cattle that I hear?"

This is one of the most penetrating rebukes in all Scripture. Understatement makes it so. Samuel could have walked in with guns blazing: "God told me last night that you disobeyed! You took the plunder. Look at all these sheep and cattle. You spared the king. You have sinned against God!"

Instead he calls attention to the "smoking gun," letting the evidence bleat the condemning truth.

Ironically, understatement emphasizes a point. "I am a Jew, from Tarsus in Cilicia, a citizen of no ordinary city," said Paul to the Roman guards.

"Dying is bad for you" — Russell Baker.

"Nothing in life is so exhilarating," said Winston Churchill, "as to be shot at without result."

Understatement is a national sport for the British, while overstatement — hyperbole, exaggeration — is the American preference. Chuck Swindoll combines hyperbole and understatement to humorous effect in his sermon, "Reasons To Be Thankful":

> When my wife and I were at Dallas Seminary back in the early 1960s, we lived in a little apartment that was a part of a small group of apartments that have since then been destroyed, I am happy to say. Hot and cold running rats — all the joys of home were there. In the summer the weather came inside, and it was hot. Hot? Hotter than you can imagine. Like a desert.
>
> That hot fall, we began to pray for an air conditioner; we didn't have one. I remember through the cold blowing winter — strange! — we were praying for an air conditioner. Through December, January, and February, we told nobody, we made no announcement, we wrote no letter; we just prayed.
>
> The following spring, before we were to have another summer there, we visited my wife's parents in Houston. While there, one morning the phone rang. We hadn't announced our coming; it was for a brief visit with her folks and mine before we went back to seminary. The phone rang, and on the other end of the line was a man I hadn't talked to in months. His name happened to be Richard. . . .
>
> I said, "How are you?"

He said, "Great! Do you need an air conditioner?"

I almost dropped the phone. [Up to this point Swindoll's delivery has been typically enthusiastic. Before the following line, however, he pauses and then calmly says,] "Uh, yes."

"Well," he says, "we have just put in central air conditioning here, and we've got this little three-quarter-ton air conditioner that we thought you might like to have. We'll bring it over and stick it in your trunk and let you take it back, if that's okay."

[Again Swindoll pauses and answers calmly,] "That'll be fine, Richard. Bring it on over."

We put that thing in the window, and we froze winter *and* summer in that little place![12]

As Swindoll did here, when using understatement, the extra incongruity of using overstatement in tandem can help listeners "get it."

Overstatement can be humorous: "Always do right. It will gratify some people and *astonish* the rest" — Mark Twain. It can have an edge to it: "If your right eye causes you to sin, gouge it out and throw it away . . . if your right hand causes you to sin, cut it off and throw it away" (Matt. 5:29,30).

Explaining understatement or hyperbole to listeners is a mistake. Much of the impact comes from listeners getting it for themselves, and if they don't, explaining only highlights your failure.

ARTISTIC SOUND: RHYME AND ALLITERATION

Alliteration — using proximate words that begin with similar sounds — accents comparison or contrast: "This time through a similar whirlwind God brings not *ruin* but *revelation*, not *disaster* but *disclosure*."

When we alliterate the key words of a sentence — the subject and verb, the verb and the direct object, a series of parallel words — the words fit and the sentence sounds right.

"If you accept Christ, righteousness can be a reality."

"His career was ruined through laziness and lying."

"The end of sin is sorrow."

Alliteration does yeoman duty in titles and outlines: "Bistro Blues," a *Time* article; "Unlistened-to Lessons of Life," a sermon by Leith Anderson.

Alliteration is both a tool and a temptation. We've all abused alliteration in sermon outlines, forcing words to fit the scheme, even at the risk of confusing the meaning. If we find we have to explain an alliterative outline for it to make sense to listeners, we've probably gone too far.

Rhyme gets attention but has limited use. It is effective in the title or skeleton of the message, where people expect and occasionally enjoy a bit of cleverness or wordplay. For example, John Guest used rhyme effectively in the sermon title "Pain Is the Name of the Game."

OTHER TECHNIQUES

Turned phrases — based on movie, book, or television titles, clichés, familiar quotes, Bible verses, or advertising slogans — draw an effective contrast: "How many times have you heard it said that in this world it's not what you know but who you know that counts? And that is often true. But in God's world, it is not what you know but who you *are* that counts."[13]

Turned phrases make for arresting titles:

"When the Roll Is Called Down Here" — Fred Craddock
"Glory to God in the Lowest" — Bruce Thielemann

One general rule of good communication is keep it simple. Sometimes, though, saying something in a roundabout way can be more interesting. It's called periphrasis.

Many biblical phrases could be shortened, but the periphrasis appeals to the heart and imagination. Instead of saying, David loves me, God says, "I have found David son of Jesse *a man after my own heart*" (Acts 13:22).

Describing a source for one of Shakespeare's plays, instead of saying, "a disorganized play," Northrop Frye, in his book *On Shakespeare*, says, "A messy dog's breakfast of a play."

One common structure for periphrasis is a hyphenated or quote-enclosed phrase used as an adjective: "They lived in a cockroaches-have-the-right-of-way tenement house."

Wordplay can be used for serious purposes. Jack Hayford described in one sermon a divine message he received regarding his finances: "The reason things are so tight is because you're too tight."

Wordplay can highlight a comparison or contrast. "You're very careful about your *actions*," said one preacher. "Character is revealed by your *reactions*."

Wordplay in sermon titles can promise communication marked by creative energy.

> "Sense out of Nonsense" — David Peterson
> "Doubts in Belief" — Paul Borden
> "Levi's Genes" — Vic Pentz

Explaining a wordplay, or any artistic element, patronizes listeners. While clarity is a virtue in communication, so is subtlety, which allows listeners the pleasure of figuring things out. Jesus regularly dropped challenging bits of teaching into the laps of listeners and left them to solve the puzzle.

"For I am convinced that neither death nor life, neither angels nor demons, neither the present nor the future, nor any powers, neither height nor depth, nor anything else in all creation, will be able to separate us from the love of God that is in Christ Jesus our Lord" (Rom. 8:38 – 39).

If redwood-solid substance like this — expressed with contrast, repetition, parallelism, balance, variation, and climax — could be written by an apostle who said, "I may not be a trained speaker, but I do have knowledge" (2 Cor. 11:6), who said he expressed "spiritual thoughts in spiritual words" (1 Cor. 2:13), who said that he "did not come with eloquence or superior wisdom" (1 Cor. 2:1), who clearly could never be accused of putting style over substance, then the lesson for us is that we don't have to choose substance over style or style over substance. For as biblical writers such as Paul and David and Isaiah and John knew, in the hands of serious communicators, artistic style *is* substance.

10

Pacing

Good pacing is like a heartbeat. With it, lifeblood flows to every capillary of the sermon. Without it, there's a good chance somebody's dead.

Ironically, listeners may be lifeless even when the sermon's pulse races from beginning to end. Several years ago I sat with my father watching a fiery missionary evangelist on TV. With a high speed, all-stops-out delivery, he addressed a conference of ten thousand people with thousands more watching by satellite.

When the sermon was over, I asked my dad what he thought of the message. "After a while, I got numb," he said. "When a preacher emphasizes everything, he emphasizes nothing."

Indeed, the preacher said, "Turn with me to John chapter ten" as urgently as "Only Jesus can save us from our sins."

As a result, this potentially great sermon was merely good. Although the preacher was passionate, his message never peaked, never crescendoed in emotion or content. Instead of a series of mountainous peaks and valleys, the sermon was one high plateau, flat on top.

What his sermon lacked was pacing. Pacing a sermon is controlling its elements — their order, length, development, and type — to maintain interest and maximize impact.

Writers are obsessed with pace. As we've mentioned more than once, they compete for attention with television, whining children, and nagging to-do lists. Writers assume the easiest thing for readers is to close the book. Unlike preachers, who can control pace to some degree with voice and delivery — raising and lowering pitch and volume, speeding up and slowing down, pausing — writers can rely only on written words.

But that's all skillful writers need. After reading chapter one of a good novel, the reader is lured irresistibly to chapter two, and not by accident. Authors know exactly what drives the reader on. They deftly modulate characterization, description, scenery, plot, and dialogue to propel readers forward, hungry for more, emotionally engaged.

Good sermon pacing does likewise. Pacing rids the sermon of dead spots, controls its emotional rhythms, and helps it hold a listener's curiosity for the duration. Preachers can learn from writers four lessons about hearty, healthy pacing.

BALANCE SLOW- AND FAST-PACED ELEMENTS

The goal is not to rid the sermon of slower-paced material. Rather, we want to vary the heartbeat.

In fiction writing, describing scenery and characters slows the pulse. Rather than wear down readers with paragraphs of description, skillful writers limit description to a few sentences or weave it into the action. "Peter pursued the burly mugger across the wide, white beaches."

Sermons also have slow- and fast-paced elements. To listeners a five-minute story runs, while a five-minute definition crawls.

Slow-paced material addresses the intellect. It is abstract, generalized, factual, analytical. Definitions, principles, Hebrew and Greek word studies, analysis, deductive reasoning, exegesis, explanation, and description are generally slower paced.

Fast-paced elements address the heart. They appeal to emotions, personal interest, the will, the imagination. They are specific, concrete, visual, personal. In general, rapid-pace elements include stories, illustrations, exhortation, challenge, application, and humor.

These are general guidelines, though. Theology done passionately will seem fast. And stories can be told in a way that feels slow — as do many of Garrison Keillor's stories, for instance. The categories given, though, usually work as we're suggesting, and so must be balanced in a sermon.

Notice how Jay Kesler achieves such balance in his sermon "Why I Believe in the Church." He begins with a philosophical argument of a famous Christian thinker.

> We have in history a man with whom most of you are familiar, a philosopher and mathematician named Pascal. He put forth something we commonly call Pascal's Proposition, and this proposition to his atheist friends went this way.
>
> He said, "Suppose you are right and I am wrong." (Pascal was a believer.) "Suppose God didn't make the heavens and the earth. Suppose mankind is just a coincidental, cosmic joke and has no purpose or reason on earth. He dies like a dog."
>
> "I've believed otherwise. And by faith in him and through his grace, I've been forgiven my sin. I've believed that, but (let's suppose) it's all false. We both die. None of the promises are true. You die. I die. Annihilation.
>
> "But, suppose I'm right and you're wrong. Suppose there is a God. We both die. Then you find yourself in a sinner's hell. But I am the recipient of the promises of God through faith. In both cases, you have everything to lose and nothing to gain, but I have everything to gain and nothing to lose."
>
> I believe in the church because it deals with these issues.

Kesler then immediately changes the pace:

> I like all kinds [of novels], but the ones I like [best] are the novels like *Watership Down*. In *Watership Down* we have a group of rabbits. Their warren is going to be destroyed by a bulldozer, and a subdivision is going to be built where they live. So we have a little rabbit, who's like Moses, going to lead them to this place called Watership Down, to the Promised Land. . . . [1]

When we have control of pacing, we needn't fear using a slow-paced, decrescendo element. The key is to be brief, and to sandwich it between fast-paced material. We can serve a healthy diet of doctrine, exegesis, Scripture exposition, and word study, if we make sure that faster elements follow slower ones.

Slow-paced material can serve well as the first step toward a climax, just as a baseball pitcher's slow curve makes his next fastball seem that much faster.

African-American preachers often start sermons low and slow. Judging by the first ten minutes, you might say they are boring. But then the preacher begins climbing the mountain. He knows from the beginning that the peaks will come, so he doesn't fear the foothills.

DEVELOP ELEMENTS IN PROPER MEASURE

In one sermon I've preached often, I tell Joseph's story from Genesis in my own words, taking almost ten minutes. After my wife had heard this message several times, I asked her if she had any constructive criticism on the sermon.

"I don't think you need to go into so much detail when you tell Joseph's story," she said. "It really slows the sermon down."

We control pace by how thoroughly we develop material. If we spend too long on even a fast-paced element, like a story, it becomes tedious. If we move briskly through a slow-paced element, the sermon's heartbeat remains strong.

Fred Craddock, in his sermon "The Hard Side of Epiphany," appears at first to spend too long talking about his family's nativity scene, but he has a purpose:

> All of our decorations are . . . from Luke. Madonnas that we've picked up here and there in travel — of wood, one of corn shocks, of brass, one of glass. They're wrapped in tissue and put back in a box like you'd put away crystal or china because they're fragile.
>
> Our nativity scene is really cheap, but the kids made it years ago. It gets prettier every year. But it's from Luke: straw, a baby, Mary and Joseph, and some animals. Sits on top of the television. . . .
>
> We have angels, all kinds of angels, around the house, on the mantle. They're from Luke. When we put them away, one of them I have to be careful not to store in a place that gets hot in the summer because the face is wax. It's from Nuremberg, Germany, and we don't want it to get messed up.

Satin dress. It's almost female, though you know how angels are. . . .

All of our decorations are Lukan. We put them away today. When I finish class and go home, that's what we'll do.

Luke is over now and we go to Matthew. Exit the women; in come the men. Exit the stable, now it's a king's palace. Exit the shepherds, enter the wise men from the East. Exit the angels, and in comes Herod.

We have a little music box. It plays carols — "Silent Night, Holy Night" and "O Little Town of Bethlehem." Just open the lid and it starts playing. It's on the coffee table. It's Lukan. Music is from Luke.

Put the lid down on that because exit Mary, enter Rachel. Exit lullaby, enter the scream: "I heard a voice in Ramah. It was Rachel weeping for her children."

It's just so hard to accept that the gospel has enemies, that good news has enemies, but there it is. Herod intimidated, and all Jerusalem troubled. . . . [2]

What at first seems like a long, sentimental digression serves a larger purpose. The nativity description set a tone of sweetness, hope, peace, and family — a tone shattered by Herod's slaughter of the infants. The contrast is powerful, enabling us to *feel* how inconceivable it is that the world hates the good news.

EMPLOY COMPLICATION AND RESOLUTION

After speaking for five minutes, a Connecticut pastor noticed his listener's eyes getting the ceramic look. He fought to hold their attention, intensifying his delivery, preaching louder, soliciting "amens." After a momentary rally, his listeners fell back into torpor.

The pastor became more animated, waving his arms, pounding the pulpit, stalking the podium. He successfully jolted his listeners into attention, though they were captivated more by his delivery than by his message.

Five minutes into his sermon, a Florida pastor faced similarly bored listeners. Instead of turning up the delivery heat, however, he uttered one sentence, no more than twenty words, that riveted the attention of every breathing soul in the room.

What kind of sentence was it? A complicating sentence. Complicating sentences and paragraphs have great power to stir interest and curiosity.

Complication — a conflict, a problem, a question — is like a pacemaker's jolt to the heart. A smoking volcano is a complication. An angry spouse, a theological paradox, a moral conflict, or a dead body are complications. Whatever makes listeners curious, anxious to resolve some tension, or intent on what happens next is complication. With complication speakers draw a mental string taut.

Let's go back to Kesler's sermon, "Why I Believe in the Church." It begins with complication, decrying our pluralistic society's attitude toward the body of Christ:

> There's a kind of paternalism about the church, that the church is a subgroup in our society, not unlike. . . the Amish. To many people, the church is sort of quaint. In the words of the great American theologian Frank Sinatra, "I'm for whatever gets you through the night," meaning people need something. And if some folks want to be quaint and come to church and listen to some religious music and get themselves jazzed up about God — if that helps them, fine. If other people want to do it with drugs or golf or whatever, that's fine too.
>
> Then there's that great number of PBS programs as well as editorials that have asked the question, "Is the church relevant?" I don't know about you, but one thing I don't want to be is quaint. I don't want some bus load of tourists pulling up in front of my house to take pictures of me like I'm Amish. I don't like the idea of having people ask the question "Is the church relevant?"
>
> I'd like to try to answer that from a personal viewpoint because I don't consider myself to be quaint, nor do I consider myself the kind of person who fools himself about relevance in culture.[3]

Kesler is angry. Listeners sense conflict between what the world thinks and what Scripture says — and Kesler passionately believes — about the church. After the introduction, listeners ache for a strong statement about the relevance of the church.

Resolution, in turn, satisfies the hunger created by complication. In one sermon, I relate how I moved to Arlington Heights,

Illinois, in 1987 to pastor a church of thirty-five people. Although prospects looked bleak — our weekly offerings fell two hundred dollars below break-even, we worshiped in a grade school gym, and the congregation suffered low morale — I moved there confident God would reverse the tide.

"Six months later," I say in the sermon, "our attendance had dipped to thirty, visitors rarely attended, and the offerings had fallen even lower. After one particularly discouraging Sunday, I lay on my bed, sweltering in the July heat, profoundly disillusioned. 'Lord, what's going on?' I prayed. 'I was sure you led me here.'"

At that point, I turn to Hebrews 10:36, which serves as my text. But the first dozen or more times I preached that sermon, I overlooked a necessary element. I told the beginning of the story for the sake of complication, preparing the way for the resolution of Hebrews 10:36. But I never finished the Arlington Heights story.

My oversight didn't go unnoticed. After the sermon, someone would usually ask, "Well, what happened in Arlington Heights? Did things ever improve?"

Listeners crave resolution. They have to know the rest of the story (which was six more months of little fruit in Arlington Heights before the church began to grow).

Complication and resolution, perhaps the best kept secret of storytellers, complement one another like hunger and food, fatigue and sleep, dissonance and harmony, itch and scratch. Complication keeps readers turning pages late into the night; resolution leaves them satisfied when they turn out the light.

Resolution is nowhere near as satisfying if not preceded by complication. What preacher hasn't proclaimed with passion the hope and blessedness of the gospel and wondered why listeners were unmoved? Well, perhaps they weren't hungry. We may have shortchanged complication, a sure path to a sermon that makes listeners feel like we're "preaching at" them instead of communicating words of life.

"He who is full loathes honey," says Proverbs 27:17, "but to the hungry even what is bitter tastes sweet." The moral for preachers: invest as much time honing complicating sentences and paragraphs as crafting principles and outlines.

One of this era's greatest preachers has lived by this principle. Billy Graham's sermons paint a gloomy picture of man's need and then offer salvation through faith in Jesus Christ. The bigger the problem, the more wonderful the answer.

The following examples of complicating sentences or paragraphs taken from sermons and magazine articles hint at how many ways there are to awaken curiosity in listeners.

Problem. From a 1991 article analyzing the Persian Gulf War: "General H. Norman Schwarzkopf had a very big problem."

Nothing subtle here. Immediately every reader wants to know what Schwarzkopf's big problem was.

Conflict. A 1993 *Sports Illustrated* article about baseball's Carlton Fisk said, "He returned to the White Sox this year after a rancorous off-season."

With a first sentence like that, most people will read the rest of the paragraph. Whether it's a sporting event, military conflict, or sibling rivalry, conflict can no more be ignored than can a fist fight in the supermarket.

False assumption. From a *Sports Illustrated* article on a Miami-Syracuse football game: "The other supposed advantage of playing at home in the Dome is the din created by the Syracuse crowd."

Words like *supposed, should have, seemed, apparently*, and *presumably* tip off the reader that conventional understanding is about to be challenged.

Assertion that begs explanation or defense. R.C. Sproul says in one sermon, "Not long ago, I talked to a man who teaches in the graduate school of Harvard University. This professor, whose specialty was the philosophy of the history of science, said to me in casual conversation that in his judgment, the universe was created by chance.

"I said, 'I'm not sure I understand that. How could the universe be created by chance when chance can do nothing?'"

Listeners to Sproul have to wonder, *What do you mean, "Chance can do nothing"? Explain that!*

Potential action. From another Gulf War article: "The young sergeant is lying prone in the sand, the butt of his M-16 rifle tucked against his shoulder."

Readers wonder, *Is he being attacked? Is he a sniper? Who is in the cross hairs of his gunsight? Who is about to live or die?* They have to keep reading to find out what happens next.

Emotion. The first sentence of another magazine article says: "English soccer fans are devastated."

Readers wonder what caused the emotion, and what actions will result. Emotions are like weather systems: They always bear watching.

Coined phrase. From William Manchester's biography of Winston Churchill: "He had begun to understand the Maginot mind."

We've heard of the Maginot line, but what is "the Maginot mind"? New catch phrases intrigue readers.

Information withheld. From a 1992 *Sports Illustrated* article about Michael Plant, who sailed solo across the Atlantic: "But Plant had reason to be apprehensive about the seaworthiness of his boat."

Immediately we wonder, *what were the problems with his boat?*

Surprise. Haddon Robinson begins one sermon, "One of the more difficult responsibilities I have as the president of Denver Seminary lies in reading my morning mail."

Few would classify opening the mail as a "difficult responsibility," so listeners want an explanation.

VARY SERMON ELEMENTS

Several years ago a man spoke several times at the church I pastored. His sole means of sermon development was to read a verse, repeat and restate a phrase or two, then exhort listeners to heed:

"'Let us love one another,' says 1 John 4:7, 'for love comes from God.' Let us *love* one another. Let us meet one another's needs. Do you spend all your time thinking about yourself and never about others? That's not love. Make up your mind that this week you're going to live a life of love!"

That's direct and effective in proper measure. His first message lasted twenty minutes and covered a long text. It was a relatively brief challenge that invigorated the congregation. But when he returned a few months later and followed the same pattern, this time for thirty minutes, he wearied the congregation.

When overused, any method of sermon development becomes tedious. Just as a symphony is paced by alternating instruments — first the soothing violins, then the rousing brass, then the haunting and fragile woodwinds, the different timbre and feel of instruments giving variety even when the theme recurs — so varied sermon development strengthens the pacing of a sermon.

Like the exhorter just described, most preachers have tendencies, favorite "instruments," ways of developing a sermon that are second nature. Some pastors spend most of the sermon telling stories. Others major in exegesis, word study, and explaining principles. Others challenge listeners and denounce cultural evils.

If you recognize monotony in development as a personal pacing problem, experiment with other instruments from the orchestra, some of which are explanation, restatement, analogy, definition, quotation, cross references, original language word study, historical background, application, challenge, principle, personal reaction, description, argumentation, negation, classification, statistics, story, warning, rebuke.

Analyzing one's own sermon orchestration pays big dividends. By listening to tapes of my own sermons and classifying sentences/paragraphs by sermon element, I've become aware of my tendencies. I do the same with other communicators to learn new ways of using the huge symphony orchestra at my disposal.

There are few things preachers dread more than the sagging interest of listeners. Few things are more precious to them, therefore, than skillful pacing.

Good pacing requires that we use the four methods of this chapter, but something more is needed: intuition. Healthy pacing comes from having a feel for the rise and fall of the sermon, a feel that comes from being sensitive to our listeners, to ourselves, to the Spirit, and to the sermon. When we are sensitive to pacing, before our listeners begin to droop, we will sense the message dragging. Before our listeners are inspired, we will sense the engaging interest and relevance of what we're saying.

A homiletical version of Proverbs 4:23 might read, "Above all else, guard your heart rate, for it is the wellspring of a sermon's life."

11

Finishing Strong

I had thought will power and adrenalin would get me through my first marathon — on time and in style. But they failed me at mile twenty. I had trained for months. I ran the first half of the race with grace and elan. But in the next seven miles I slowly began to falter. By mile twenty I was ready to give up. To this day, I'm not sure why I didn't. As I ran the last six miles my legs shook, my head ached, and my stomach rolled.

I stumbled across the finish line fifteen minutes later than I had planned. As for style: I immediately headed for the first aid tent and lay down for ten minutes. Then I went home and vomited. Though I had trained well, I hadn't trained well enough to finish strong.

Finishing strong is a problem for preachers as well.

"The conclusion [of the sermon] is burdened with two handicaps," wrote George Sweazy, former preaching professor at Princeton Theological Seminary. "The minister prepares it when he is the most tired, and the congregation hears it when they are the most tired."[1]

This is perhaps the main reason many sermons stumble across the finish line, sometimes fifteen minutes late. After all the exegesis and exposition, we're depleted — it's just too much pain and trouble to craft a conclusion. So we hope against hope that preaching adrenalin will carry us to the end.

Sometimes it does. But most of the time it doesn't, and the weary congregation endures a spent, rundown conclusion.

As with other parts of the sermon, the ultimate effectiveness of the conclusion depends on the working of the Holy Spirit. Still, adhering to a few principles can keep us out of the way of the Spirit.

MISTAKES TO AVOID

Most of us have heard or used the illustration about the Chinese letter character that means "crisis"; we go on to point out it also means "opportunity." The illustration also applies to sermon conclusions.

One writer observes: "The closer you get to the ending, the more weight each word has, so that by the time you get to the last several words, each one carries an enormous meaning. A single gesture or image at the end can outweigh all that has gone before."[2]

The conclusion is a crisis/opportunity to leave the congregation with a lasting impression, one that can linger for days, perhaps a lifetime. So we don't want to waste it. Here, in particular, are four hazards to avoid.

First, we shouldn't conclude the sermon just one more time. After one address, William Jennings Bryan, the famous American political orator, was scolded by his mother, "Will, you missed several good opportunities to sit down."[3]

When we're not quite satisfied with the closing story, we add a closing quote, which just needs a line or two of explanation, which calls to mind a metaphor that seems to sum it all up, but lest people get confused, we summarize what we've said — and on it goes.

We are wise to remember an adage of George Sweazy: "When the time to quit has come, then every good idea is the enemy of all the others."[4] We must take the trouble to find the best idea and then leave other good conclusions for other sermons.

A second temptation is the fake ending. Again, George Sweazy has some solid advice: "In the last quarter of the sermon, a preacher must be careful to say nothing that suggests he is about to quit when he is not. Several emphatic sentences, a poem, or a powerful illustration may put the congregation in the home-stretch frame of mind. Then, when the preacher goes on, they feel betrayed."[5]

In a similar vein, many who are experienced in homiletics warn against the use of words like *finally* or *in conclusion*. Such words usually announce that you know that you're taxing people's patience. It's especially frustrating for a congregation to hear a second *finally*.

The old joke goes, "An optimist is someone who gets ready to leave when the preacher says, 'And finally, friends . . . ' " It would be nice if we could, by a firm resistance to this temptation, make this barb not so pointed.

Third, we are often tempted to conclude a different sermon than the one we started. We can't resist the moving anecdote we came across during the week. It doesn't fit in any particular point of the sermon, but, we convince ourselves, surely "it says it all." Besides, even if it doesn't fit exactly, people will love it.

Maybe we can get away with that once or twice, but a steady diet of good but irrelevant conclusions leaves congregations confused and annoyed. Better to save the great conclusion for the sermon for which it's intended.

Finally, we're tempted to use the closing prayer as the sermon's conclusion. In the prayer, we summarize the key points of the sermon and ask God to help us do what the sermon has instructed us to do. Such a prayer doesn't fool anyone: it is veiled exhortation.

As I look back, I realize I gave my congregations a steady diet of such prayers. I've also noticed two things about this practice: it doesn't work as prayer, and it doesn't work as exhortation.

If I'm going to use a closing prayer, I want my conclusion to stand without it. Then a simple concluding prayer, like the following, can do extraordinary work: "Jesus Christ, fill us with your Holy Spirit that we may be less of what we used to be and more of what we ought to be. Please, please. Amen."[6]

EIGHT WAYS TO END

One of my friends, a Lutheran, used to marvel at his pastor: "No matter his topic, at the end, he always ties it to Communion. Some weeks I've thought, No way. But he always does it. He could tie biblical genealogies to the Lord's Supper!"

Though this preacher showed intellectual dexterity, he demonstrated homiletical tedium. For my friend, the sermon's conclusion became not a moment to consider the sermon, but a puzzle: how are we going to tie this to communion this week?

This is only one problem with using the same formula week after week. The other is boredom. If congregations know what is coming, they will tune out the very part that should leave them with a lasting impression.

We ought to have in our quiver, then, more than one arrow that can send the sermon home. Here are eight that effective communicators use.

1. Summarize. Some preachers, like Karl Barth, disdain the summary ending: "If a summary is needed, it is already too late to give it; the mischief has been done."[7] Barth is partly right. If the sermon is so complicated that it needs a summary, its problems run deeper than the conclusion.

Still, a summary conclusion works well in a teaching sermon. Since listeners retain relatively little of oral presentations, it's critical to review the points of a teaching sermon, not only along the way, but also at the end.

2. Paraphrase. Here the main point of the sermon is repeated in fresh language or with a new definition or metaphor. This brings closure and reinforces the big idea without seeming pedantic.

Steve Brown uses a quote to help him redefine his main point in "The Prime Principle." He has been talking about abiding in Christ, and he concludes by saying, "Someone has said, 'Prayer moves the hand that moves the world.' That's true, but you don't move the hand that moves the world unless you've held it for a while. That's abiding in Christ."[8]

3. Circle back. Repeating or developing an image, story, or quote from the introduction gives the sermon a frame and thus a sense of completeness. Don McCullough, in his sermon "Whom Do You Serve?" begins by referring to a trip he took to Ghana, mentioning some unique expressions of the language of Ghana.

Ghana is then dropped — until the end of the message. Then McCullough says, "The Presbyterian missionary I was visiting in Ghana told me . . . "[9] He goes on to relate another Ghanaian experience that sheds light on his theme.

4. Play the refrain. If the sermon has made use of a refrain throughout, the refrain is a natural way to conclude.

In the middle of her sermon "A Theology of Baseball," Nancy Becker, starts using Yogi Berra's dictum "It ain't over 'til it's over" as a way to talk about grace. Every time she tells a story about getting a second chance, she repeats Berra's line. It also becomes the last line of the sermon: "God's love is always seeking us, always following us, always overlooking the errors and giving us still another inning, still another chance at bat. It ain't over 'til it's over."[10]

If the refrain has had emotional power in the sermon, it can provide an emotional climax in the conclusion.

5. Illustrate or quote. Stories and metaphors can bring fresh energy to the end of a message because they can appeal to the heart as well as the mind. There are as many ways to use illustrations and quotes at the end as in the middle. See chapter 5 for a review of the various uses of illustrations, quotes, and facts.

6. Quote the biblical text. In "A Breath of Fresh Air," William Hinson uses 1 Thessalonians 5:11 as one of his texts. The text is never exposited, and for good reason: he wants to save it for the end. In the meantime, Hinson tells stories showing people getting encouraged at critical moments in their lives. At the end, he speaks of Christ as "the supreme encourager. He builds us up. He believes in us even when we don't believe in ourselves. We can't stop it. We can't reverse what he did on the cross. We can only respond. 'Therefore, encourage one another and build one another up just as you are doing.'"[11]

The last sentence of a sermon already has authority; when the last sentence is Scripture, this is even more true.

7. Apply the text. Puritan sermons often followed a set outline: the first two parts of the sermon would explain the text and its doctrines; the third part would elaborate on the "uses" a text might have for everyday living. The word *uses* has gradually been replaced by the word *application*, as has the way a sermon is constructed. Few today save all the application for the end. But from time to time, it remains an appropriate way to end a sermon, particularly the doctrinal sermon.

Also under this heading would go the specific suggestions a preacher might give at the end of a sermon: if the sermon concerns civic responsibility, we often end by encouraging people to register to vote; if the sermon concerns the building fund, then the application might be for people to fill out a pledge card.

8. Challenge or appeal. "Our expectation . . . as the sermon comes to an end," writes John Stott, "is not merely that people will understand or remember or enjoy our teaching, but that they will do something about it. 'If there is no summons, there is no sermon.'"[12]

In one sense then, all sermons are a challenge or appeal to the will, even if the appeal is simply to praise God. Otherwise we're just relating interesting information. No, we want to change lives, and that means at some point, especially at the conclusion, we need to exhort people to do whatever the text would tell them to do.

That is easier said than done, though there are a variety of ways of doing it — as the next section will explain.

TEN WAYS TO TELL THEM WHAT TO DO

In an egalitarian culture, people don't like being told what to do. We like to make up our own minds, and we may label as arrogant someone who presumes to tell us how to believe or behave.

So these days we hear less straightforward exhortation, in which the preacher simply tells listeners what they should do. There are many exceptions, of course, depending on one's church tradition. In an evangelistic sermon, Leighton Ford concludes, "If God is calling you tonight, come home. Begin now. Heed that call and tonight come home where you belong."[13]

In a sermon on marriage, Stuart Briscoe concludes, "If you have a shaky marriage, don't rush off to seminars, buy lots of books, or watch videos until you sit down together and work carefully through 1 Corinthians 13, verses 4 through 8."[14]

Still, in many traditions it is rare for the preacher to use or imply the second person, "you," to address listeners. People feel we become "preachy" when we do.

Then again, that's our job! We're not giving lectures; we're proclaiming the Word of God. Many communicators in our culture, then, have had to learn how to tell people what to do without seeming to do so. Here are ten common approaches.

1. First-person preaching. If we can't often get away with a direct address in the second person, we can refer to other "persons."

We can use the first person singular, for example. Bill Hybels, in "The Story of Seven Demotions," describes the pride common to all of us, exhorting us to humility, to die to self. At the end, though, he includes himself in the indictment and appeal: "The primary purpose of this passage is to call me, someone who is intoxicated with upward mobility, to get on the wagon, to join Christian AA, to get off that drug and have Jesus' attitude. . . . "[15] Given the many examples used in the sermon, listeners know that when Hybels says "me," he really means "all of us," though he doesn't quite say so.

Or we can use the third person plural, we or us, including ourselves in the appeal. Don McCullough does this as he concludes "How Christian Is Your Tongue?": "On this day of Pentecost, let us open ourselves to the power of the Holy Spirit, who is present here. Let us open ourselves anew so that the Spirit can come in and claim us afresh, taking control of our hearts."[16]

2. Somebody out there. We can also use the third person singular, referring to some vague he or she, or to some person in the closing illustration who represents everyone. In one sermon, Bill Hybels used his conversation with an airline passenger as the main piece. After being invited to believe in Christ, the man refused, saying he wanted to think about it. Hybels then concludes the sermon, exhorting the congregation by talking about the man: "I doubt if I'll ever see that man again, but I'm praying I'll see him in heaven. . . . I hope he signed on."[17]

Or we address a collective entity like the church: "If heaven is a practical expression of Mark 3, where all of the people who do God's will are brothers and sisters and mothers, then it seems to me the church ought to practice that pattern here and now more than it does."[18]

3. Other authorities. Since some people no longer trust the preacher as an authority, we might call upon other authorities from time to time. When we quote a writer or philosopher or hymn or poem, we're saying, "Hey, this isn't just my opinion; this recognized authority also acknowledges this stuff." This is one rationale behind closing the sermon with a biblical quote.

We can do this more subtly, by appealing to people not in our name, but in God's: "Our Lord invites you today to . . . " In one sense, of course, this is all we do in preaching: announce what God is inviting people to do. If we say it plainly too often, though, it will become trite or sound presumptuous. But periodically it is a good reminder for people.

4. Lessons we can all learn. After preaching about the four creatures mentioned in Proverbs 30:24 – 28, Haddon Robinson concludes, "Four things on earth are very small. If you could sit at their feet . . . you could learn some lessons.

"From the ant you learn the value of knowing the times. . . . From the coney you understand the need to know where your security is. . . . From the locust you discover your power is in community. . . . If you have the perspective of a lizard, you see God's incongruity."[19]

He never tells us directly to trust in God or commit ourselves to church, and yet by the mere description of these lessons, he does exactly that.

5. Subtle inference. This is perhaps the most sophisticated way to end, since it requires the congregation to supply the exhortation. For that reason it can be highly effective, because it forces congregations to think about what has been said.

The main theme of William Willimon's "Don't Think for Yourself" is the depravity of humankind, and essentially he is exhorting people not to depend on their good will or human wisdom to act well in this world. Willimon concludes the sermon by saying, "The philosopher Immanuel Kant once said, 'I stand in awe of two things: the starry heavens above and the individual law of morality within.'

"I'm still awed by the starry heavens."[20]

The congregation has to fill in: "But don't be awed by or depend on your own moral abilities."

6. Promise. If we cannot get away with the stick alone, we can always add the carrot. For preachers, that means showing people not only the biblical command, but also the biblical promise.

In his sermon "Worship or Worry?" Rod Cooper concludes by combining exhortation with a promise: "Some of you may feel as if you're free falling without a parachute. . . . All I can say is relax. Do your best, knowing God has never dropped you before, and he won't drop you now. You'll discover when all you have left is God, God is enough."[21]

Many argue that this and the following point are keys to appealing effectively to the post-World War II generation, who demand to know reasons for change.

7. Consequences. We can also show that by ignoring the preached word, something worse will befall listeners. This is not the stick and carrot approach, but rather the stick and bigger stick.

In trying to help people come to grips with tragedies, Marlin Vis concludes, "[God] won't explain himself. . . . 'Blame me or trust me,' he seems to be saying. Be angry, be bitter, or be at peace. . . . It's time to stop playing the blame game. It's time to start trusting God."[22]

In "Beyond the Bottom Line," Howard Hendricks implies that things will stay the same or get worse for Christians if we don't change: "You are the salt of the earth. You are the light of the world. Christianity is languishing across this country, particularly in the marketplace, because we've forgotten why we're here instead of in heaven."[23]

This ending is in some ways stronger than second person exhortation, and yet if handled carefully, it doesn't come across as authoritarian.

8. Questions. Asking the congregation questions at the end of the sermon puts the responsibility for obedience in their hands, letting them answer the questions and decide what they are going to do.

"Every single person in this room is one heartbeat away from eternity," Stuart Briscoe concludes in one sermon. "How do you face that? How do you handle that? In what way are we helping people in their grieving and in their believing to achieve that which is of significance in their lives?"[24]

9. Hope and prayer. We can soften our admonition by putting it in the subjunctive mood, not as much commanding as expressing a hope that the congregation will change. The usual approach is to say, "I hope . . . " or "I pray . . . " or "I trust . . . "

Encouraging people to give with glad hearts, Don McCullough says, "I certainly hope we smile when we put money in the offering plate. I hope we smile knowing that we are praising God. I hope we smile because we are saying no to Mammon. May it be so for us."[25]

We can combine this with first person plural exhortation. In concluding a sermon on Ezekiel's vision of the valley of dry bones, Richard Allen Farmer says, "May there be a rattling among us. May there be a fresh wind of the Spirit among us. And may we stand as a vast army, declaring the Lord is God."[26]

10. Story, period. Sometimes a story sums up all we have to say, so that we don't even have to comment on it. It's an effective way to end, since the exhortation is entertaining and simply implied. At best, we can add the text (another authority) to drive home the point.

This is William Willimon's tack in "You Need a Good Priest," in which he argues that Christ is our great priest, someone to whom we can go with any of our troubles. He concludes,

> She was in the last stages of cancer of the lung, gasping day after day for breath, in great pain, wasted away, exhausted by fighting. She clutched in her hand each day a crucifix. It was given to her by her grandmother when she was a girl, carved by some monk in Europe. It was for her a symbol of all that her Catholic faith meant to her. When I entered the room that afternoon, I could see that she was very close to the end.
>
> "Would you like me to pray for you?" I asked. "Would you like me to summon for you a priest?"
>
> With her last ounce of energy, she held out to me in her hand that crucifix, the body of Christ nailed to the cross. She said, "Thank you. But I have a Priest."

Then Willimon simply added, "Let us therefore approach the throne of grace with boldness so that we may receive mercy and find grace to help in time of need."[27]

Of course, many sermons combine these ten approaches. In three sentences, Bill Hybels uses four of these methods at the end of "A Better Kind of Grieving." He concludes, "What are you going to do? Which way are you going [questions]? The stakes are very high [consequences]. I hope you make the right choice [subjunctive], and so does God [another authority]."[28]

Author Don McKinney said to writers, "The ending is probably the second most important part of your article, after the lead."[29] The same applies to sermons.

No matter what our tone or approach, we are wise to craft the conclusion carefully. In fact, given the crisis and opportunity that the conclusion presents — remember, it will likely be people's lasting memory of the message — it's probably a good practice to write out the conclusion, regardless of how much of the rest of the sermon is written.

By the way, one other piece of advice about endings fits well here: "When you're ready to stop, stop."[30]

12

Preaching Within Yourself — and Beyond

My drive from the second tee sliced sharply and bounced lazily into a strand of oaks. When I found my ball, I faced a not uncommon challenge: just ahead stood two oaks, whose branches touched but whose trunks stood ten feet apart. To hit the green, I was going to have to thread my shot under and between these trees.

To my left was a clear pitch to the fairway. But a pitch meant defeat, a bogey at best. The potential par lured me forward.

So did the golfing greats. On TV I had watched Jack Nicklaus and Arnold Palmer and Lee Trevino (this was a few years ago) slip shots between narrow openings. I reasoned that if the pros did it that way, I should too.

I aimed and swung. A direct hit to the right. The ball glanced back, hopped past my foot, and came to rest a few yards behind my original lie.

Undaunted — *Even the pros blow it once in a while,* I reasoned — I set up and aimed for the narrow gap again. The ball hit a branch and careened right — deeper into the woods. After a few more desperate swings, I found myself putting for a triple bogey.

I missed.

Had I accepted my level of skill (I wasn't exactly a seasoned pro), had I not tried to slavishly imitate others, I would have sacrificed a stroke and chipped onto the fairway. I would have finished the hole with a respectable bogey, or a double-bogey at worst.

One of the great temptations of preaching — especially after reading a book that highlights the Jack Nicklauses of preaching — is to try immediately, all at once, to imitate the greats. This will make for triple-bogey preaching at best.

All communicators have to learn this lesson. Writers certainly do. An aspiring essayist spends days reading a fine writer, let's say Pulitzer prize-winning Annie Dillard. She admires her compact prose, her unusual metaphors, her attention to detail. So she decides she's going to write like Dillard. But when she does, her prose ends up stilted, forced, pompous.

To resist the temptation to be anybody but yourself I've gathered in this last chapter some advice from accomplished writers and preachers, and one golfer — advice on how to take what has been said in this book and use it wisely.

DO IT WITH STYLE — YOURS

Every communicator has a style, a certain way of developing ideas, forming sentences, crafting language, using words. Regarding style, William Zinsser's advice to writers in his modern classic *On Writing Well: An Informal Guide to Writing Nonfiction* applies to preachers. He says that style is organic to the writer; it is as much a part of him as his hair, or his lack of it. Adding style is like adding a toupee. Though at first glance the formerly bald man looks young, perhaps even attractive, a second look (and with a toupee, he notes, there is always a second look) suggests something is wrong. He is well-groomed all right, but he just doesn't look like himself.

Zinsser concludes, "This is the problem of the writer who sets out deliberately to garnish his prose. You lose whatever it is that makes you unique. The reader will usually notice if you are putting on airs. He wants the person who is talking to him to sound genuine. Therefore a fundamental rule is: be yourself.

"No rule, however, is harder to follow. It requires a writer to do two things which by his metabolism are impossible. He must relax and he must have confidence."[1]

OFFER *YOUR* GIFTS

Confidence comes partly from experience. After a few hundred sermons notched in the pulpit, you know you can give a passable sermon, no matter the circumstances. Funerals pile up and committees proliferate and community obligations mount and the family is in turmoil — we know weeks like that — and still we eventually learn how to preach passably on Sunday morning.

Confidence also comes when we fathom this simple truth: God loves me and has a wonderful plan for my preaching.

Each preacher brings a unique history, personality, and perspective into the pulpit. This is no accident. It's called providence. You have been born at a particular time, to particular parents, in a particular place, enduring particular experiences, coming to conclusions particular to you.

You are the unique thing you bring to the pulpit. Certainly you aim to interpret the text faithfully, and you want to preach Christ and not yourself. But it is *you* who preaches Christ. And you will preach Christ a little differently than any other preacher. Not to do so is to deny your God-given uniqueness.

Every preacher should be able to identify with the thoughts of writer and teacher Dorothea Brande on this matter: "If you can come to such friendly terms with yourself that you are able and willing to say precisely what you think of any given situation or character, if you can tell a story as it can appear only to you of all the people on earth, you will inevitably have a piece of work which is original."[2]

And if you can preach biblical sermons as they appear to you of all people on earth, you will inevitably preach originally and effectively.

EXPERIMENT

How you find your pulpit self is not a matter of simply being yourself in the pulpit. You have to discover, of all the preaching styles available, which best fits you. The key to finding that style seems to be experimentation.

"In this regard," writes Richard Neuhaus in his *Freedom for Ministry,* "a certain amount of imitation is inevitable in the process of discovering one's pulpit personality. . . . Billy Graham, Fulton Sheen, Robert Schuller, William Sloane Coffin, and Clarence Jordan have no doubt been 'done' in thousands of pulpits across the country. Better — because it reduces the risk of appearing ludicrous — to imitate a less well-known preacher."[3]

As we try out various techniques of the masters, we learn our strengths and weaknesses, and we can adapt accordingly.

One Sunday morning I read, word for word, a sermon by John Henry Jowett. Although it didn't electrify the congregation, I found myself entranced with his turns of phrase, his strong, vigorous verbs, and his precise nouns. I knew afterward that the crafting of the sermon's language would become a larger part of my preparation.

On another occasion, I preached a sermon imitating the style and tone of Dietrich Bonhoeffer's *Cost of Discipleship.* I was firm, authoritative, prophetic, and all that stuff. I was also boring. I discovered I don't do prophetic well.

Sometimes, though, what you can't do well at one time, you can, after a few years' experience, pull off. Once I returned from a conference at which narrative preaching was the rage. For two weeks I crafted narrative sermons from the Gospel of John, telling each story from the eyes of one of the characters in the biblical account. The third week, for lack of preparation time, I reverted back to my usual, didactic style. At the door, one woman commented, "I'm glad we didn't have to hear another cute story today."

I put narrative preaching away after that. But it continued to intrigue me. I read and reflected on this style of preaching for some years. After a great deal of study and experimentation (in writing) with the art of storytelling, I tried another narrative sermon, this time during a brief Good Friday meditation. One person was so impressed that she said, "You certainly have the gift of preaching."

Well, I don't know if I'd say that, but I do work at it, and once in a while it sounds like I'm gifted, especially when an experiment finally comes off.

Then again, sometimes it comes off, but you wish it hadn't. Before one conference for junior high youth, I left my face unshaved for two weeks. My scraggly appearance on the first day of camp elicited a few stares from campers and counselors alike. I began my first talk by shaving, stressing how we shouldn't judge by first impressions. Everyone liked it, but I blush to this day about using such a gimmick. I blush even more when I hear that other pastors have done the same thing — and worse — from their pulpits.

"Experiment definitely does not mean the introduction of novelties and entertainments to compensate for the failure of preaching," writes Neuhaus. "It does mean that the preacher is conscious of his craft and deliberative about the ways in which a change of tone or gesture or illustration can better effect communal engagement."[4]

KEEP IT SIMPLE

With all the rhetorical tools sitting before us on the homiletic workbench, we are tempted to use each and every one of them on our next sermon, trying to produce a sermonic masterpiece to be remembered for the ages.

This is especially tempting on important occasions. George Sweazy, former professor of homiletics at Princeton Theological Seminary, notes that few things are more disastrous than the attempt to preach a great sermon. When the preacher strives for greatness, that's just when he falls on his face. Sweazy concludes, "We might think that great preaching requires an exalted topic, a mind-staggering conception, and sublime thought. But the best sermons have a limited topic, a crystal-clear conception, and down-to-daily-life thought. A minister's Easter sermon is often his poorest. . . . Stylishness is the enemy of style."[5]

Instead, we are wise to use these tools to the degree that they fit our gifts and personalities. (I've mentioned my inability to pull off prophetic sermons.)

Our level of preaching maturity is another factor to consider. Recently I used this line in a sermon: "Though the waste seemed monstrous, and though the feeling of desertion went soul-searing deep, deeper still went his trust and love." *Monstrous* and *soul-searing* are words I could not have used six years ago. They would have seemed forced, an immodest striving for style. Today they work partly because I have, over the years, integrated more dramatic language into my preaching.

In determining when and how to use the various tools at our disposal, we should aim for clarity first. Beauty and eloquence should be added to make things even more clear, not more impressive.

ONE THING AT A TIME

A golf swing is a complicated maneuver. Hands, wrists, arms, hips, shoulders, torso, knees, and feet all need to be doing things in order, in tempo. But you don't improve your golf swing by thinking of them all at once.

Cary Middlecoff, a golfing great of another era, put it this way in an old book: "As you begin each round, single out some aspect of the swing to concentrate on for that particular day. Not two; just one. Don't get your mind cluttered up with a lot of nonessentials, but don't stand there swinging with your mind a blank."[6]

That old advice for golfers is solid advice for preachers. I've found it best to attend only to one or two elements of preaching in any given sermon. Perhaps I'll work on crafting my illustrations, or maybe using strong verbs, or maybe the conclusion. In any event, I don't want to stand there preaching with my mind blank, but neither do I want to fill it with too much advice.

We'll be at this craft for a lifetime. There's no rush. Slowly, step-by-step, working on one thing at a time — that's how to build a solid preaching style.

PLAY GAMES WITH YOURSELF

When I was a pastor, anxiety bordering on panic afflicted me whenever I noticed that a classmate from seminary days was a featured speaker at a conference. *How does he rate?* I would think. I would read the brochure and eye his picture and envy would rage within.

And then there was the time I was asked to become the youth pastor of a 2,000-member church. Since I was at the time doing youth ministry in a 500-member church, it would have meant a large step up for me. But I learned some troubling news during one phone interview: the senior pastor was younger than me, and he was, according to one member of the search committee, a "dynamite" preacher.

I turned down the offer. I knew I would never be able to sit humbly at the feet of that pastor; I had my own plans for pulpit greatness.

Friendly competition that spurs one to do better is one thing. But competition that inspires jealousy is another. Unhealthy competition finally makes for a depressed preacher. Unless you happen to be the best preacher in the world, there will always be someone better; you'll always come out the loser.

Then again, we're going to have to find ways to motivate ourselves to continue to improve, and competition is one of them, if it's competition with the self.

My daughter, son, and I do pull-ups, push-ups, and sit-ups together three mornings a week. The day we started, after my son and daughter had done their first set of pull-ups, I grabbed the bar. My son said, "Now don't make us feel bad, Dad."

He was assuming two things: first, that I was going to be able to do more than his two pull-ups, and second, that we were competing. In both cases, he was wrong.

I reminded him of a truism of physical fitness: "In fitness you compete with no one but yourself. Each of us is made differently, with different levels of natural strength. Your goal is not to beat me but, over the long run, to beat yourself."

Sometimes it's that contest with the self that best keeps us motivated to preach well. At other times, measuring ourselves against an invisible audience works.

Joe DiMaggio was a great outfielder. He moved in long, graceful strides, and like all great outfielders, he made the hardest catches look routine. He also hit the ball with power, but he didn't look as if he were exerting himself.

Though DiMaggio's playing looked effortless, it was anything but that. He always gave his best effort. When a reporter once asked him about this, how he motivated himself to play so well each day, Joe said, "I always thought that there was at least one person in the stands who had never seen me play, and I didn't want to let him down."[7]

Our highest motivation is to please Christ and bear fruit for eternity with our preaching, but most of us benefit from playing such games with ourselves, whether it be competing with ourselves or pleasing some imaginary listener.

DISCIPLINE — AND MORE

Finally, Christian writer Walter Wangerin has some hard words that apply to preachers:

> I'll have not praise nor time for those who suppose that writing comes by some divine gift, some madness, some overflow of feeling.... I'm especially grim on Christians who enter the field blithely unprepared and literarily innocent of any hard work — as though the substance of their message forgives the failure of its form. FAITH HAD BETTER BE DRESSED AS BEST AND AS SKILLFULLY AS THIS WORLD DRESSES ITS LIES! For the world writes fine, fine.[8]

William Zinsser — a writer with much fine advice — puts the matter positively:

> What you write is yours and nobody else's. Take your talent as far as you can and guard it with your life. Only you know how far that is.... Writing well means believing in your writing, and believing in yourself, taking risks, daring to be different, pushing yourself to excel. You will only write as well as you make yourself write.[9]

For Christian preachers, of course, this requires something more than mere self-discipline — although there is at least that. The something more is the brooding, moving, exhilarating power of the Holy Spirit, who inspires, invigorates, forgives, and catapults our preaching. When we combine our personalities with this Gift and the many gifts in our rhetorical tool box, we will offer fine, fine preaching — a strong voice that proclaims a clear Word, a Word that convicts and redeems the world.

Notes

Chapter 1

1. Quoted in Ian Pitt-Watson, *Preaching: A Kind of Folly* (Philadelphia: Westminster, 1976), 45.
2. Pitt-Watson, *Preaching*, 49.
3. Pitt-Watson, *Preaching*, 46.
4. Pitt-Watson, *Preaching*, 47 – 48.
5. Quoted in John R. W. Stott, *Between Two Worlds: The Art of Preaching in the Twentieth Century* (Grand Rapids: Eerdmans, 1982), 273.
6. Quoted in George Sweazy, *Preaching the Good News* (Englewood Cliffs, N.J.: Prentice-Hall, 1976), 126.
7. Richard John Neuhaus, *Freedom for Ministry*, rev. ed. (Grand Rapids: Eerdmans, 1992), 156.

Chapter 2

1. Timothy Perrin, "Unleashing Your Creativity," *Writer's Digest* (July 1989): 20 – 25.
2. For more on the rationale behind freewheeling, read Peter Elbow, *Writing with Power* (New York: Oxford University Press, 1981).
3. For further reading on clustering, see Gabriele Lusser Rico, *Writing the Natural Way* (Los Angeles: J. P. Tarcher, 1983).

4. See Erika Lindemann, *A Rhetoric for Writing Teachers*, 2d ed. (New York: Oxford University Press, 1987), and Richard Coe, *Form and Substance* (Glenview, Ill.: Scott Foresman, 1981).

5. Peter Leschak and Marshall Cook, "The Five-Step Creativity Workout," *Writer's Digest* (November 1991): 26.

6. Perrin, "Unleashing Your Creativity."

7. Cited in Eleanor Grant, "A Pen by Any Name," *Psychology Today* (February 1988): 16.

8. David Ogilvy, *Confessions of an Advertising Man* (New York: Atheneum, 1988).

9. Leschak and Cook, "The Five-Step Creativity Workout," 26.

10. Denise Shekerjian, *Uncommon Genius* (New York: Penguin, 1990), 44 – 45.

11. Leschak and Cook, "The Five-Step Creativity Workout," 26.

12. Quoted in John Briggs, *Fire in the Crucible: The Alchemy of Creative Genius* (New York: St. Martin, 1988), 21.

13. John Ortberg, *Leadership* (Summer 1993): 39.

Chapter 3

1. William Zinsser, *On Writing Well*, 3d ed. (New York: Harper & Row, 1985), 65.

2. Haddon Robinson, "Good Guys, Bad Guys, and Us Guys," *Preaching Today*, no. 80.

3. Jill Briscoe, "Yet Will I Praise Thee," *Preaching Today*, no. 52.

4. Howard Hendricks, "The Message of Mistakes," *Preaching Today*, no. 54.

5. Bruce Thielemann, "Christus Imperator," *Preaching Today*, no. 55.

6. Dale Rosenberger, "Fear Vanquished," in Michael Duduit, ed., *Great Preaching 1991* (Jacksonville, Fla.: Preaching Resources, 1991), 17.

7. Paul R. Adkins, "And They Laughed at Him," *Pulpit Digest* (March – April 1992): 56.

8. Larry Reibstein, "Where the Jobs Are," *Newsweek* (January 20, 1992): 42.

9. Joel Gregory, "The Forgotten Man of Christmas," *Preaching Today*, no. 100.

10. Bruce Thielemann, *"When Life Crowds You Out,"* Preaching Today, no. 95.

11. Thomas Steagald, "Two Divided by Two," *Great Preaching 1991,* 33.

12. John Schwartz, "The Highway to the Future," *Newsweek* (January 13, 1992).

13. R. C. Sproul, "The Insanity of Luther," *Preaching Today,* no. 49.

14. Richard John Neuhaus, *Freedom for Ministry* (San Francisco: Harper & Row, 1979), 161.

Chapter 4

1. Andy Stanley, "Conviction Versus Preference," *Preaching Today*, no. 98.

2. William Zinsser, *On Writing Well* (San Francisco: Harper & Row, 1976), 62.

3. John Stott, "Freedom," *Preaching Today*, no. 102.

4. John Killinger, "Be Still and Know That I Am God," *Preaching* (July – August 1991): 10.

5. Stuart Briscoe, "What About Shaky Marriages?" *Preaching Today*, no. 89.

6. Terry Fullam, "Life on Wings," *Preaching Today*, no. 96.

7. Richard John Neuhaus, *Freedom for Ministry* (San Francisco: Harper & Row, 1979), 157.

8. Bruce Thielemann, "Because," *Preaching Today*, no. 105.

9. Fred Craddock, "When the Roll Is Called Down Here," *Preaching Today*, no. 50.

10. Don McCullough, "Gratitude," *Preaching Today*, no. 95.

11. Haddon Robinson, "The Wisdom of Small Creatures," *Preaching Today*, no. 93.

12. Annie Dillard, *The Writing Life* (San Francisco: Harper & Row, 1989), 7.

Chapter 5

1. Maxie Dunnam, "I Am the Door," *Preaching Today*, no. 53.

2. B. Clayton Bell, "How Do You Catch the Wind?" *Preaching Today*, no. 81.

3. John Maxwell, "God Gives Through People," *Preaching Today*, no. 34.

4. "To Illustrate," *Leadership* (Winter 1985): 48.

5. Dunnam, "I Am the Door."

6. Jim Dethmer, "The Gift of Mercy," *Preaching Today*, no. 112.

7. Charles Swindoll, "Reasons to Be Thankful," *Preaching Today*, no. 50.

8. Dethmer, "The Gift of Mercy."

9. John Huffman, "Meeting Your Family's Material Needs," *Preaching* (September – October 1992): 43.

10. Bruce Thielemann, "Legions of the Unjazzed," *Preaching Today*, no. 36.

11. William Willimon, "Don't Think for Yourself," *Preaching Today*, no. 114.

12. Calvin Miller, "The Mind of a Servant," *Preaching Today*, no. 51.

Chapter 6

1. Terry Fullam, "Life on Wings," *Preaching Today*, no. 96.

2. Stuart Briscoe, "What About Shaky Marriages," *Preaching Today*, no. 89.

3. Bruce Theilemann, "Glory to God in the Lowest," *Preaching Today*, no. 75.

4. Howard Hendricks, "Charge to Dr. Joseph M. Stowell IV," *Preaching Today*, no. 70.

5. Haddon Robinson, "The Wisdom of Small Creatures," *Preaching Today*, no. 93.

6. Robinson, "The Wisdom of Small Creatures."

7. *Preaching Today*, no. 80.

8. Joel Gregory, "He Cannot Be Hid," *Preaching Today*, no. 85.

Chapter 8

1. Annie Dillard, *The Writing Life* (San Francisco: Harper & Row, 1989), 70.

2. William Strunk and E. B. White, *Elements of Style,* 3d ed. (New York: MacMillan, 1979), 23.

3. Peter Marshall, "Were You There?" *Preaching Today*, no. 103.

4. Jeremiah Wright, "The Audacity to Hope," *Preaching Today*, no. 82.

5. Andrew Perves, "Forgiven: The Evangelical Indicative," *Pulpit Digest* (September – October 1991): 66.

6. John Killinger, "The Nourishing Quiet," *Preaching* (July – August 1991): 10.

7. John Killinger, "Entertaining Mystery," *Pulpit Digest* (November – December 1992): 13.

8. James Lowry, "By the Waters of Babylon," *Journal for Preachers* (Easter 1992): 27.

9. Haddon Robinson, "The Wisdom of Small Creatures," *Preaching Today*, no. 93.

10. Adapted from Strunk and White, *Elements of Style,* 67.

Chapter 9

1. Bruce Thielemann, "Tide Riding," *Preaching Today,* no. 30.

2. Walter Wangerin, "An Instrument of Peace," *Preaching Today,* no. 35.

3. George Munzing, "Living a Life of Integrity," *Preaching Today,* no. 32.

4. John Hannah, "Is There Any Comfort?" *Preaching Today,* no. 50.

5. Richard Corliss and Richard Schickel, "Why the Christmas Films Don't Sparkle," *Time.*

6. Thielemann, "Tide Riding."

7. Munzing, "Living a Life of Integrity."

8. Haddon Robinson, "Good Guys, Bad Guys, and Us Guys," *Preaching Today,* no. 80.

9. Hannah, "Is There Any Comfort?"

10. Winston Churchill, speech about Dunkirk before the House of Commons, June 4, 1940.

11. James Melvin Washington, ed., *A Testament of Hope* (San Francisco: Harper & Row, 1986), 219.

12. Charles Swindoll, "Reasons to Be Thankful," *Preaching Today,* no. 50.

13. Munzing, "Living a Life of Integrity."

Chapter 10

1. Jay Kesler, "Why I Believe in the Church," *Preaching Today,* no. 37.

2. Fred Craddock, "The Hard Side of Epiphany," *Preaching Today,* no. 39.

3. Kesler, "Why I Believe in the Church."

Chapter 11

1. George Sweazy, *Preaching the Good News* (Englewood Cliffs, N.J.: Prentice-Hall, 1976), 100.

2. Jerome Stern, *Making Shapely Fiction*: quoted in Don McKinney, "The Big Finish," *Writer's Digest* 72 (February 1992): 42.

3. Quoted in Donald E. Demaray, *An Introduction to Homiletics* (Grand Rapids: Baker, 1990), 129.

4. Sweazy, *Preaching the Good News*, 101.

5. Sweazy, *Preaching the Good News*, 101.

6. John Claypool, "The Future and Forgetting," *Preaching Today*, no. 109.

7. *Homiletics*, trans. Geoffrey W. Bromiley and Donald E. Daniels (Louisville: Westminster/John Knox Press, 1992), 127.

8. Steve Brown, "The Prime Principle," *Preaching Today*, no. 107.

9. Don McCullough, "Whom Do You Serve?" *Preaching Today*, no. 110.

10. Nancy Becker, "A Theology of Baseball," *Preaching Today*, no. 115.

11. William Hinson, "A Breath of Fresh Air," *Preaching Today*, no. 114.

12. John R. W. Stott, *Between Two Worlds: The Art of Preaching in the Twentieth Century* (Grand Rapids: Eerdmans, 1982), 246.

13. Leighton Ford, "Hope for a Great Forever," *Preaching Today*, no. 96.

14. Stuart Briscoe, "What about Shaky Marriages?" *Preaching Today*, no. 89.

15. Bill Hybels, "The Story of Seven Demotions," *Preaching Today*, no. 103.

16. Don McCullough, "How Christian Is Your Tongue?" *Preaching Today*, no. 106.

17. Bill Hybels, "Christianity's Toughest Competitor," *Preaching Today*, no. 115.

18. Howard Vanderwell, "Christian Singles," *Preaching Today*, no. 99.

19. Haddon Robinson, "The Wisdom of Small Creatures," *Preaching Today*, no. 93.

20. William Willimon, "Don't Think for Yourself," *Preaching Today*, no. 114.

21. Rod Cooper, "Worship or Worry?" *Preaching Today*, no. 108.

22. Marlin Vis, "The Blame Game," *Preaching Today*, no. 114.

23. Howard Hendricks, "Beyond the Bottom Line," *Preaching Today*, no. 101.

24. Stuart Briscoe, "Encouraging People to Look Ahead," *Preaching* (May – June 1993): 32.

25. McCullough, "Whom Do You Serve?"

26. Richard Allen Farmer, "A Trip to the Valley," *Preaching Today*, no. 113.

27. William Willimon, "You Need a Good Priest," *Preaching Today*, no. 106.

28. Bill Hybels, "A Better Kind of Grieving," *Preaching Today*, no. 108.

29. Don McKinney, "The Big Finish," *Writer's Digest* 72 (February 1992): 45.

30. William Zinsser, *On Writing Well: An Informal Guide to Writing Nonfiction* (San Francisco: Harper & Row, 1976), 79.

Chapter 12

1. William Zinsser, *On Writing Well: An Informal Guide to Writing Nonfiction* (San Francisco: Harper & Row, 1976), 20 – 21.

2. Dorothea Brande, *Becoming a Writer* (Los Angeles: J. P. Tarcher, 1934, repr. 1981), 120 – 21.

3. Richard John Neuhaus, *Freedom for Ministry* (San Francisco: Harper & Row, 1979), 150.

4. Neuhaus, *Freedom for Ministry*, 168.

5. George Sweazy, *Preaching the Good News* (Englewood Cliffs, N.J.: Prentice-Hall, 1976), 126.

6. Cary Middlecoff, *Advanced Golf* (Englewood Cliffs, N.J.: Prentice-Hall, 1957), 18.

7. From Zinsser, *On Writing Well*, 238.

8. From Kathryn Lindskoog, *Creative Writing: For People Who Can't Not Write* (Grand Rapids: Zondervan, 1989), 233.

9. Zinsser, *On Writing Well*, 238.

Index of
Persons Cited or Quoted

(Numbers in *italic* type indicate persons identified in the endnotes and not in the text.)